JUST FOLLOW the SIGNS

DANIEL G. MUELLER

SERMONS FOR ADVENT, CHRISTMAS, & EPIPHANY

Series B (Gospel Texts)

C.S.S. Publishing Company
Lima, Ohio

JUST FOLLOW THE SIGNS

4851/ISBN 0-89536-676-2

Table of Contents

Author's Preface

A healthy controversy developed in England in the late 1800s over a newspaper editorial that criticized a particular pastor's preaching. A parishioner wrote in complaining about the fact that he had faithfully attended worship services at his church for over fifty years and in all those years he could not remember a single sermon he had heard. By his estimation, the preacher had done nothing to inspire him.

For several weeks subsequent editorials appeared, some supporting the complaint and some trying to defend pastors and preaching. Nothing that appeared in the newspaper was sufficient to quiet either side until one editorial which was written by a sincere person who failed to sign his name. He wrote simply, "I have been married to the same woman for the past fifty years. In all those years she has faithfully prepared my meals day after day. I cannot, in all honesty, say that I remember any specific menu she ever prepared. Sometimes I can't even remember what we ate just yesterday. All I know is that day after day, year after year, she has given me nourishment and I thank God for it." Following the appearance of this editorial, there were no others on the subject of preaching.

As you go about the business of nourishing your congregation through preaching, it is my prayer that this material will be of service to you and that it will give glory to God. The Lord bless you and your ministry.

— Daniel G. Mueller

Advent 1
Mark 13:33-37

Ready or Not, Here I Come!

There's an amusing commercial on TV in which a man is about to let go of his bowling ball as he eyes the pins at the end of the lane. Just as he is ready to release the ball, he gets lifted out of himself by two men in sparkling white suits and goes walking off across the lanes, through the walls of the building and onto a staircase surrounded by clouds. At first he doesn't understand what in the world is going on but then it suddenly dawns on him. He has just died. He looks at the two white-suited men at his side and asks in disbelief, "Are you sure it was supposed to be me? I was working on a string of strikes!" Convinced there was no mistake, he goes off reluctantly and shrugs, "Gee, I guess I just wasn't ready." The point of the commercial is that one has to be ready all the time and for the sponsor that means having insurance, a "piece-of-the-rock." That's the way to be ready.

"I guess I just wasn't ready!" There's no way to say that without feeling bad. Students say it when they stare at a big, bright red "F." Baseball batters lament it as they slouch off to the dugout after yet another strikeout. Hunters complain about it as they relive in their minds that big buck that got away while the safety was still on. "I guess I just wasn't ready."

Sometimes the consequences of not being ready are truly tragic. Consider the case of the young man and the young woman, just divorced, who look at each other through tear-filled eyes and confess, "I guess I just wasn't ready for marriage." If only that had been their foresight and not their hindsight. When Freddie Prinze, the actor on TV's "Chico and the Man," committed suicide several years back, his agent tried to explain it by saying, "I guess he just wasn't ready for success." Being ready is a good thing. Not being ready is bad news.

Of all the things there are that we need to be ready for, the most important of all is the Day of the Lord, Judgment Day. In our Gospel lesson our Lord Jesus instructs all who are his disciples always to be ready for the Day of his return. "Take heed," Jesus warned, "Watch. Be alert. Stay awake. Don't get caught sleeping. Always be ready for that day when I come back for you."

Jesus is coming back! The same Lord who was born a Babe in Bethlehem, who lived and died on the cross in payment for the world's sins, then came back to life again and ascended into heaven, is coming back. At the Ascension, when Jesus returned to heaven, two angels said to his disciples who watched him go, "This same Jesus who was taken up from you into heaven shall return in like manner." (Acts 1:11)

Over and over again the Bible tells us the good news that Jesus is coming back and each time it also tells us to be ready for his appearing. Our Savior explained why he is coming back: "I go to prepare a place for you, and when I go and prepare a place for you I will come again and take you to myself that where I am you may be also." (John 14:3) Jesus is coming back to take us to himself, to our eternal home.

When that will happen, no one knows. Jesus said, "Of that hour and that day no one knows, only the Father in heaven." (Matthew 24:36) So, the Savior continued, "Always be ready because I am coming at an hour you do not expect." (Matthew 24:44) In describing the sudden unexpectedness of his return, Jesus compared the day of his coming to lightning which bursts out of the sky without warning (Matthew 24:27) and to the arrival of a thief who always comes when nobody thinks he will. (1 Thessalonians 5:2)

We don't know when, but we do know that Jesus is coming back. "You will see the Son of Man coming in the clouds of heaven," Jesus promised. (Matthew 26:64) "Everyone will see the Son of Man coming in a cloud with power and great glory," he said. (Luke 21:27) "Every eye will see him, even those who pierced him." (Revelation 1:7)

Jesus is coming back. It would be good to us to be ready for him. Of all the worst possible times, this would be the worst of all to say, "I guess I just wasn't ready." In Revelation Jesus speaks to

John in a very visual way about the urgency of always being prepared. "Behold, I come as a thief," he told John. "Blessed is he who watches and keeps his clothing so that he will not have to walk around naked and ashamed in public." Don't get caught with your pants down, Jesus said. Be ready, Be prepared! (Revelation 16:15)

The way to be ready is to be about the Lord's business, to be doing what God wants us to do. Jesus compared it to a man going away on a trip and leaving his servants in charge of all his business. The man who went away is Jesus when he ascended into heaven. The servants he left behind to carry on his business are we, all who believe in him. When we are about his business, we will be ready. If we ignore his business, we will be unprepared. In the Gospel of Luke, our Lord Jesus spoke about this very bluntly, precisely, and to the point. "Watch yourselves," he said. "Don't become so occupied with the things in this world that the Day comes on you suddenly and finds you unready for it, for it will come like a trap on all people over all the earth. Be on watch and pray always that you will have strength to go safely through all these things that will happen and to stand before the Son of Man." (Luke 21:34) Don't get so wrapped up in the things of this world, Jesus admonished.

The Savior gave us a perfect illustration. "Remember the days of Noah," he said. "Back in those days before the Flood, everybody was eating and drinking and marrying and giving in marriage." Noah was doing those things too, but at the same time he was also building an ark, he was doing God's work for him. When it began to rain, he got into his ark with his family and was saved; everybody else missed the boat. Watch! Be ready!

To be ready does not mean to separate ourselves from life, to climb up on some mountain someplace and just wait. No, we continue living; but as we do all that we do, we do it as God's people, his servants who carry out his business as we wait for him to return. (Matthew 24:38)

This is a tremendously important message for us, the busy-busy-people, to hear. Soon Christmas will be upon us. As we make ourselves ready for Christmas, what will we do? Well, we have to shop for presents; plan parties; send Christmas cards; mail out-of-town gifts; hide the presents from the children; get a Christmas tree and decorate it; put up the lights outside the house; we have all kinds of things to do. But having done them all, will we be ready to celebrate God's tremendous gift of his Son to be our Savior? Where will God's work have been done in all that other stuff? Will we also set aside some special time to pray and to meditate and to share with each other the wonder of God's great love for us, a love so great he gave us his only Son? Or will we get to Christmas and be so tired by then that we can't even sing "Joy To The World" and mean it? Most people get ready for Christmas by spending too much money and exhausting themselves. Then the good news of God's wonderful gift doesn't do anything for them because they are too worn out to hear it.

Jesus was right! The world is a trap for us because we get so wrapped up in it. That's why he died. Jesus died so that the world might be crucified to us and we to the world. (Galatians 6:14) He died so that we might be in the world but not of the world. He died to keep us unspotted by the world. "I have chosen you out of the world," Jesus said. (John 15:19) We don't know how to get ready for Christmas. Will we be ready for him when he comes back to us?

We will be if we are about the Lord's business. And his business is this: that we confess our sins and believe that he is our Savior who died for all; and that we live no longer for ourselves but for him who for our sake died and was raised. (2 Corinthians 5:15) We are ready when we have a piece of the Rock — not insurance, but God, our Rock of Refuge, our Redeemer. "Behold, I come quickly," Jesus said. "Hold tightly to what you have" (the gift God has given you) so no one takes your crown." (Revelation 3:11) The way children hang on for dear life to those special presents they get, taking them to bed with them and never letting them get out of their hands; the way those presents make all the others they got seem like nothing; that's the way we are to cling for all we are worth to Jesus Christ alone and not be sidetracked from him. St. Paul was ready for the Lord's return. He confessed, "For me to live is Christ . . .!" That's the way to be ready.

"Ready or not, here I come!" Jesus is ready. Scripture tells us the day of the Lord is near. We are ready also, by grace through faith, when we live in him who lived and died and rose again for us, in him and for him, the One who is coming to take us to himself. Amen

Advent 2
Mark 1:1-8

Cultural Revolution or Spiritual Problem?

Can you imagine what it would be like if John the Baptizer were the pastor of this congregation today? I wonder who would run away first, John or all the rest of us? The way the Scriptures decribe him, it sounds as if he would have been very hard to get along with. The man could never have come to your home for dinner, for instance, because he ate only locusts and wild honey. Most of you ladies don't know how to fix locusts, I don't think. He never drank any alcohol so he would have been no good at a cocktail party. He was loud and probably obnoxious. He looked like a "weirdo," going around in a coat of camel's fur. If he were our pastor we'd probably be embarrassed to death if we ever had to introduce him to any of our friends.

Worst of all, he was always talking about sin, harping at people, preaching repentance over and over again. He even did that to the king. John does not sound very attractive; and yet the Scriptures say about him, "There was a man sent from God, and his name was John . . . " (John 1:6)

While John may not sound very attractive by description, nevertheless there was something about him that attracted people to him. Mark tells us that all of Judea and all the people in Jerusalem came out to see him. Multitudes of people were attracted to him and believed what he had to say because they were baptized by him. All kinds of people came — tax collectors, soldiers, Pharisees, Sadducees, Temple priests — they all came asking John what to do and they listened to what he told them.

One could attribute John's popularity to a charismatic personality perhaps. Every once in a while a person comes along with such a magnetic personality that everyone automatically looks up to him. John Kennedy was like that. Whether he did good or bad didn't matter all that much to most people. People just plain *liked* him. And one could say that John the Baptizer was of that charismatic type also.

Maybe. But there was a great deal more to it than that.

John was a man sent from God with a specific job to do. Writing for God, Isaiah prophesied that John would come and explained what he would do. "Behold, I send my messenger before your face, who shall prepare your way; the voice of one crying in the wilderness, 'Prepare the way of the Lord . . . ' " John was sent from God to get people ready for the arrival of God's Son, the Savior of the world, Jesus Christ. God prompted people to flock to John so that he could prepare them for the good news of salvation.

In the play, "Godspell," a modern retelling of the good news of Jesus Christ, John the Baptizer is the first character on stage. The play begins with him, much as God's plan of salvation began to be unfolded *through* him. In the play, John appears on stage dressed like a circus ringmaster. One gets the message that his job was to "get the show going." As "Godspell" begins, there is a beautiful song which John sings. The melody is haunting and the words repeat over and over again, "Prepare, ye, the way of the Lord . . ."

John was special from the very beginning. St. Luke, whom tradition tells us was a doctor, relates an incident in the early life of John that shows how powerful God's influence on him was from the very start. When John was still in the womb of his mother Elizabeth, in about the sixth month of pregnancy, Mary, pregnant with Jesus, came to visit Elizabeth. The two women were relatives. When Mary came close to John's mother, John leaped within his mother's womb. Those of you who have been pregnant can appreciate the wonder of such acrobatic activity. He jumped inside the womb, Dr. Luke explains, because when he heard the voice of the Savior's mother he recognized her to be the mother of the Lord. Luke knew about babies moving around in the womb. He also knew that John was chosen by God, before time began, to do a job for the Lord.

John's purpose in life was given to him by God. All that God expected from John was that he do what God wanted him to do. God put him at the right time and the right place to do it. Our purpose in life is given to us by God as well. He has put us in the right place at the right time for us. All he expects of us is that we obey him. When we do, he promises to fulfill his purpose for us. (Psalm 56:2)

John's God-given purpose in life was to prepare the way of the Lord. He did that by preaching sin. John preached sin with enthusiastic abandon. He called the people who came out to him "vipers" and condemned their insincere religion. "Bear fruits that befit repentance!" he shouted. Don't just *say* you are sorry for your sins. *Show* it!

John's goal in preaching sin so harshly was not to humiliate people, but rather to shake them out of the idolatry of believing in themselves and their good works. He wanted to show them how desperately they needed a Savior. Having convinced them of their sin, he pointed out to them the solution to their problem by pointing at Jesus and announcing, "Behold, the Lamb of God, who takes away the sin of the world." From John, the people not only heard about their damning iniquity, but also about God's redeeming love, his deliverance in Jesus Christ the Savior.

The proclamation of sin is as valid today as it was in John's day. Sin has not stopped being a problem. It is still an inherent part of every human life. The good news of salvation in Jesus Christ still begins with the bad news of sin. There are some who would preach sin less and God's love more. We need to preach God's love as much as possible, but it will have no meaning at all if we do not also preach sin. To fail to preach sin is to place an obstacle in the way of the Gospel.

It's a mistake to make light of sin. Our Lord Jesus thought it was pretty serious stuff. In fact, from some of his miracles one gets the distinct impression that he thought it was our greatest problem. Jesus always forgave sin first and then healed sickness. As bad as infirmity is, sin is far worse, because sin kills.

Instead of addressing the real problem of sin, we have developed a tendency in these latter days to sugar-coat the problem with our language. We speak instead of cultural revolutions. People living together before marriage is not a sin problem, they argue, but the result of our cultural revolution. As part of the cultural revolution that we are experiencing right now, we are suffering from an erosion of respect for authority. Nobody wants to respect authority anymore. Children do not respect parents, teachers or anybody else. Adults do not respect the boss, the spouse, or the government officials. This is not a cultural problem but a spiritual one. It is sin.

Perhaps one of the worst indicators of sin in our lives is the fact that we almost never stop to ask if something is right or wrong any more. We only ask if it "feels good," is convenient, expedient or easy. Especially in our use of technology, we do this. Our technology has expanded so wondrously that we can do all kinds of near-miracles now. Babies are conceived in test-tubes! We can do these things, but we have often not stopped first to ask whether they are right or wrong.

Paul wrote a catalog of sin to describe Roman society nearly 2,000 years ago. What was happening back then has not changed much. Listen: Homosexuality, wickedness, evil, covetousness, malice, envy, murder, strife, deceit, gossip, slander, hatred of God, insolence, haughtiness, boastfulness, invention of evil, disobedience to parents, foolishness, faithlessness, heartlessness, ruthlessness. (Romans 1:26-31) These are not cultural dilemmas. They are sin.

John preached *repentance* for the forgiveness of sins. Repentance is nothing less than owning up to the reality of our sinfulness. Some people define repentance as turning away from sin, not sinning anymore. If that's the case, then no one has ever truly repented, for we sin over and over again until we die. True repentance is a turning away from a careless attitude about sin. Repentance means turning away from believing that sin is not a problem and confessing that it is indeed *my* problem. The unrepentant in John's day were the Pharisees who said they had no sin; the repentant were all those who confessed their sin.

Many people came to John confessing their sin. That's the way to handle the problem. It does no good to pretend sin isn't real, to try to cover it up. Adam and Eve tried to hide from God after their first sin; they hoped God would not see them. They tried to cover their nakedness, their sin, with fig leaves. But the fig leaves didn't do the job. They didn't work. There is no way to deny the reality of sin. But, when we confess it, God is faithful and just and forgives us. He covers our nakedness, our sin, with the sparkling robe of Christ's righteousness.

Because God lives in us who believe in his Son Jesus as our

Savior, we know there is no way to hide from him. We don't even try. We confess, "O God, have mercy on me, a sinner." Mercy is precisely what God gives us for the sake of Jesus, the "Lamb of God who takes away the sin of the world." In his precious name, we thank God that such mercy is so freely given. Amen

Advent 3
John 1:6-8 and 19-28

It's not what you know, but who you know!

In a dark room, pitch black except for the glaring light from the naked bulb of a small lamp set on a table, there are three men. One, bedraggled and covered with sweat, sits at the table, his face exposed to the light. Standing next to him are the two other men who move in and out of the light, sometimes shoving their faces right into the face of the man who is seated.

No doubt you have watched enough TV dramas to know what's happening in that room. The man seated is being interrogated. "Where were you on that night?" he is being asked. "What were you doing?" "Who were you with?" "Why should we believe you?" Questions keep hitting him from all sides because his interrogators want to get all the facts. The expression on the seated man's face indicates it is not a pleasant experience.

John the Baptizer must surely have felt as though he was being interrogated that day when the priests and Levites, sent by the Pharisees in Jerusalem, shot questions at him. "Who are you?" they asked. "What are you? Why are you doing what you are doing? Are you Elijah? Are you The Prophet? Give us an answer . . . What do you say about yourself?" Like detectives interrogating a suspect, they questioned the Baptizer, wanting to get all the facts, wanting to know everything, wanting to understand, so they could approve or disapprove of him.

For John it was all very frustrating. He wanted to give them the facts they needed to know. He wanted to share with them the good news he had. But they asked all the wrong questions about the wrong person. They were getting lost in details. John tried to confess his faith, but they were too busy asking questions to hear what he had to say. "You don't know Jesus," he told them. "You don't need to know about me. All I am is a voice crying in the wilderness, 'Prepare the way of the Lord.' You need to know Jesus, for he is so much greater than I am that I am not even worthy to untie his sandals." It's not *what* you know that counts, John tried to tell his questioners, but *who* you know. People need to know Jesus. John's interrogators did not know him. We all need to know Jesus. It is horrible *not* to know him. Not knowing him keeps us from getting to what really counts in life. We can be close to it and yet far away.

In Samaria one day, thirsty, Jesus sat down by a well and waited to get a drink. Presently a woman of the region came by. She knew all about the details of drawing water. She knew what a hassle it was to go to the well every day to replenish her supply. She knew how tired she was of the whole routine. She even knew that Jesus needed help from her, because he didn't have anything with which to draw water. She knew all these things. But she did not know Jesus.

Jesus offered to give her living water, water welling up to eternal life. But she was so lost in the dreary details of drawing water from a well that she completely missed the wonder of his offer. "Sir, give me this water," she said, "that I may not thirst nor come here to draw water any more." (John 4:15) The greatest good she could think of at that moment was not to have to bother with that stupid well ever again. She did not know Jesus. He revealed himself to her as the Messiah, the Savior; and she learned from the Lord about the very greatest thing: a new and eternal life in him. Then she knew Jesus and suddenly everything in her life began to count much more, making sense and meaning more than ever before. That only happens when one knows Jesus.

We want to know all kinds of things. We want to know what is happening in the world and what is going on in our neighbor's house. But unless we also know Jesus, we might as well know nothing at all. The prophet Jeremiah wrote, "Let him who glories, glory in this: That he knows me and understands me that I am the Lord who exercises loving kindness, judgment and righteousness in the earth." (Jeremiah 9:24) There is no greater good than to know Jesus.

There was a young man long ago who thought he knew everything. He knew all the Commandments of God. He even thought he knew all about Jesus. He came to Jesus one day asking a question to which he thought he already knew the answer: "What do I have to do to be saved?" The Lord gave him the answer he expected to hear: "Keep the Commandments." Smugly, the young man thought to himself, "I knew that." He told Jesus he had been keeping them all since his youth. The man did not know Jesus, nor did he "know it all," because what Jesus then said to him completely eroded his self-confidence: "Sell all you have, give it all to the poor and then come follow me." The young man was not ready to hear that; he could not do that; and went away full of sorrow.

We know more today than ever before. There is a temptation to think that we don't need to know about God anymore. Some even say, "I know too much to believe in God!" When Jesus visited Nicodemus late one night, he said to him, "You don't know how the wind happens." (John 3) Today we know all about the wind. We know all about high pressure and low pressure, different kinds of clouds, wind chills, wind shears, and jet streams. King Solomon, in all his wisdom, did not know how babies come to be formed in the womb. Like all the other people of his day, he thought mothers had nothing to do with it, that fathers pass complete little babies into the mother's womb and all the woman does is incubate them for a while. We know a great deal more about how babies happen. We know all about fertilization, cell division, and gestation. We even have pictures of it happening. We know far more now, but it is still true that unless we know Jesus we might as well know nothing at all. "And this is life eternal," Jesus said, "to know you, the only true God and Jesus Christ whom you sent." (John 17:3)

We know far more today than used to be known. People even say about their children, "The kid knows more than I do; I never knew that when I was her age!" Do you know that since the beginning of recorded history the accumulation of all our knowledge has doubled six times? And it is projected that in the next fifty years it will again double thirty-two times? I've heard it said that unless people continue to learn regularly in their field of expertise, in just eight years their knowledge will be completely outdated. We know much more now.

Some of our new knowledge is wonderful. Think of the advances in medicine, the way doctors are able to repair eyes, rebuild joints, even exchange hearts and other parts of the anatomy. Think of how much easier it is to travel now than it was just fifty years ago. Some of our new knowledge is not so wonderful, however. Think of the bomb and how much easier we can now kill one another and destroy the earth. Our Supreme Court is supposed to be filled with knowledge, but some of their recent decisions that protect the criminal and harass the victim simply boggle the mind and make us wonder what happened to their knowledge.

Knowledge, all by itself, is not a blessing. Unless it develops within the context of knowing God it can even be dangerous. The more educated one becomes the greater the likelihood seems to be of falling away from the faith. I remember in my early years of college thinking how "cool" I was because I thought there was no God. "In their wisdom, they become fools . . . " is how St. Paul described it. (Romans 1:22) Fools say there is no God. (Psalm 53:1) The solution is not to stop gaining knowledge, nor to stop learning, but rather to learn in the context of knowing God most of all. "Add to your faith virtue," St. Peter wrote, "and to virtue add knowledge" — the knowledge of God. (2 Peter 1:5) "The fear of the Lord is the beginning of wisdom," the Scripture says.

In the final analysis, our knowledge of God is the only thing that is going to count. What matters is our knowledge of him and our faith in him. It is God who reveals the deep and secret things. Only God knows what is in the darkness. It is only God with whom the light dwells. (Daniel 2:22) When we walk through the valley of the shadow of death, as we do so many times throughout our life, what will then comfort us will not be *what* we know, but *who* we know. Even if the doctor knows all the probabilities and shares them with us, it will still only be our knowledge of God that will comfort us. Job walked through that dark valley, losing all his children, his possessions and his health. Still, he confessed, "I know that my Redeemer lives . . . " (Job 19:25) That Redeemer and the knowledge of him sustained Job. Nothing else could have. St. Paul, also, persecuted and humiliated for the sake of the Gospel, confessed to his son in the faith, Timothy, "I know in whom I have believed and I am persuaded that he is able to keep that which I have committed to him safe in that day." (2 Timothy 1:12) Neither man knew as much as you and I do. They both believed the world was flat. Yet they knew all they needed to know. They knew Jesus.

By the grace of God, you and I know Jesus also. From childhood on we sing, "Jesus loves me, this I know." Thank God for the wonder of that. We possess the greatest knowledge of all: We know God! We know him not because we discovered him but because he found us and saved us. God has made himself known to us through his Holy Spirit. He came to us in the water and word of Holy Baptism. He comes to us daily through his written and spoken word. He comes to us in bread and wine, the Body and Blood of his Son. And we know him. We truly know him. Along with our knowledge of him, we also "know that we have passed out of death into life" (1 John 3:14) because of him.

There is no greater knowledge than this, no matter how many details we can ever know. Thank God, we know it, in Jesus' name. Amen

Advent 4
Luke 1:26-38

Lessons From A Girl In Trouble

Mary was "in trouble." A married woman gets pregnant and we say that she "is in a family way," or "expecting." But when an unmarried girl gets pregnant, we say she is "in trouble." And Mary was definitely "in trouble." She was going to have a baby and she wasn't married.

One day, out of the clear blue sky, with no warning or advance preparation whatsoever, an angel from God came to Mary and told her she was going to have a baby. The news was understandably frightening and startling. Mary wondered what in the world was going on. But the angel said to her, "Do not be afraid, Mary, for you have found favor with God. And behold, you will conceive in your womb and bear a son and you will call his name Jesus." It was the kind of news that can wake one up very fast.

For Mary this news was confusing. "How can this be," she asked, "since I have no husband?" What she meant is that she had never had intercourse with anyone. "How can I have a baby without that?" she wondered. The angel explained, "The Holy Spirit will come upon you, and the power of the Most High will overshadow you . . . " That's how it was going to happen. And Mary, the Virgin, became pregnant. Or, as it seemed to those who knew her, she "got into trouble."

Had her pregnancy resulted in the usual way, she would indeed have been "in trouble." But her pregnancy was unique, unlike any other that has ever happened. She got pregnant not due to some indiscretion, but as a direct result of God's willful plan for the salvation of the world. She got pregnant because she found favor with

God and because God chose her, in his grace, to "be blessed among all women." She got pregnant because God was bringing his only-begotten Son into the world through her.

Mary was not the only one affected by the angel's marvelous news and its development. Her parents, about whom we are told nothing, surely must have suspected their daughter, wondering what in the world she had been up to. She was engaged to a man named Joseph, and Scripture tells us he not only suspected the worst, but was ready to act on his suspicions. One can hardly blame the poor man. Mary had gone away to the hill country of Judea to visit her relative Elizabeth, who was also pregnant. She was gone three months. Shortly after she got back the tell-tale signs of her pregnancy began to show. Joseph jumped to some logical conclusions: Mary had been unfaithful.

It took an angel from God to change his mind. After Joseph had prepared himself quietly, and with as much kindness as possible, to break off his relationship with Mary, an angel came to him and told him to go ahead with his plans to marry the girl, because that which had been conceived in her "was of the Holy Spirit." It was all part of God's promise, the angel told Joseph, his wonderful promise through Isaiah: "Behold, a virgin shall conceive and bear a son and his name shall be called Emmanuel, which means, God with us." (Matthew 1:23)

Jesus, our Savior, was born of a virgin. This is part of the marvelous mystery of our faith, part of the good news that St. Paul labeled "a scandal." For many people, the virgin birth is simply too fanciful a thing to believe. It is unacceptable, some say, because it sounds too much like mythology: gods coming down from heaven to have babies with human girls. Whatever it sounds like, it is a biblical fact. Jesus, our Savior, was born of a virgin.

The virgin birth is only half the story, however. We also confess that he was "conceived by the Holy Ghost." The Father of Jesus was God himself, the Holy Ghost. And because of it, the angel could say about the baby that would be born of Mary, "He will be great and will be called the Son of the Most High . . . the child to be born will be called holy, the Son of God." Jesus, the baby born in Bethlehem, was true human, born of the Virgin Mary, and true God, conceived by the Holy Ghost. He was holy, blameless, undefiled and separate from sinners. He was made higher than the heavens. (Hebrews 7:26)

It was a miracle, a true miracle! Unlike so many things which are labeled miracles in our day, things which are nothing more than God's customary grace at work, the birth of our Lord was a true miracle. By definition, a miracle is a break in the laws of nature. When a virgin gives birth, that's a break in the laws of nature — much like when a man walks on water or a dead man comes back to life.

The birth of God's Son, our Savior, is nothing more than popular history for us until we confess it, with head and heart, as part of our faith. Until we believe it, it's just something that happened a long, long time ago. The same is true of Jesus' Baptism, that time long ago when God said from heaven, "This is my beloved Son with whom I am well pleased." When we confess it, it stops being "just history" and becomes part of God's good news for every day of our lives. Listen to what John wrote: "Whoever confesses that Jesus is the Son of God, God abides in him and he in God." (1 John 4:15) God lives in him and he lives in God. God is with him and he is with God. And that's what the birth of Jesus is all about, isn't it: God with us. That happens when we confess him. Then we have good news for every day of our lives.

In the miraculous birth of our Lord there are some good lessons to learn, lessons that will help us live each day of our lives to God's glory and our benefit. There are two lessons especially for us to note. The first is *obedience;* the second is *trust.*

God wants us to obey him. Mary and Joseph obeyed God. It surely must not have been easy for them to do that. There must have been a lot of hassles in their life. What God asked of each of them was extremely demanding. But they obeyed God. Joseph did what he was given to do and Mary did what God gave her to do.

Ever since Eve's decision to disobey God we have been faced with a constant battle to obey him. The temptation is always there to do what *we* want to do instead of what *God* wants. We like to decide for ourselves what is right and wrong, what is good and bad. In every aspect of life we struggle with obedience.

A recent movie entitled, "Right of Way" addresses the issue dramatically. In the film, James Stewart and Bette Davis play an elderly couple who decide to commit suicide because they can't bear the thought of living without each other. What God has to say about the sanctity of human life doesn't matter. All that counts is what they want.

If this were just a film, that would be bad enough in itself. But the film is more and more frequently becoming a true story as greater numbers of people begin to accept suicide as a viable alternative. There is no obedience in such a decision.

Suicide is just one example. If we check any area of our life and hold it up to God's commandments, we can find examples of how we disobey God, seeking to ignore his will in favor of our own.

Beyond faith, what God wants from us more than anything else is obedience. No matter how difficult or unpleasant a task he lays before us, God wants us to obey him. "Be doers of the word and not hearers only," we read in his Word. (James 1:22) It isn't easy to obey, but of all there is that we could ever give to God, our finest gift is obedience to his will. (1 Samuel 15:22) "If anyone loves me," Jesus said, "he will keep my words . . . and my Father will love him and we will come unto him and make our abode with him." (John 14:23) Jesus nowhere promises obedience will be easy; But he does promise that the Father will love us for it.

Jesus obeyed God. "I have kept my Father's commandments and abide in his love," he said. (John 15:10) Jesus was perfectly obedient in our place, *for us,* to earn forgiveness for us because of our disobedience. Now Jesus, the Obedient One, lives in us to make us obedient like him. He was "obedient unto death, even death on a cross" for our sakes. (Philippians 2:8) He prayed, "Not my will but thine be done," and has taught us to pray and to live the same way.

The second lesson is *trust.* We are to trust God the way Mary and Joseph did. Mary's trust was so complete that she told the angel after hearing all he had to tell her, "I am the slave of the Lord; he can do with me whatever he wants!" Can you hear yourself saying that? "I am the slave of the Lord, he can do with me whatever he wants!" When I can't find a job; when the doctor wants to do surgery; when my spouse doesn't give me any affection any more; in every trial of life? Trust God with the trust of Mary: "I am the slave of the Lord; he can do with me whatever he wants."

Trust him because he is the God who does the impossible, who made a virgin have a baby. Trust him because he is the God who brings good out of bad things. Mary got into trouble; how awful. Through that, God brought the Savior Jesus into the world; how wonderful. Trust God because he works for good in all things with those who love him. Mary trusted in God and was rewarded with the gift of the Savior, a gift the Virgin shares with us, with all who trust in God.

"Don't be afraid," the angel told Mary. God says the same to us. Do not be afraid to obey and to trust me. I will never let you down for I am with you always. I gave my Son as a living guarantee of that fact. Amen

Christmas Day
John 1:1-14

The Chief Miracle of Christmas

Three little boys were playing together one day. In the course of their play they began to speak about their fathers. Actually, they began to brag about their fathers, each trying to make his father bigger and better than any other father in the whole world. They bragged about a number of things until they came, finally, to brag about the most important thing of all (in their eyes): how much money their fathers made. The first little boy, whose father was a lawyer, boasted, "My Daddy makes so much money that we get to buy a new car every year." The second little boy, the son of a doctor, replied, "Oh, yeah? Well, my Daddy makes so much money that he's always telling my Mommy that she can't *spend* it fast enough." The third little boy was the son of a preacher. He was quiet for a moment as he thought and thought about how he could win this discussion. As his two friends looked to him for his rebuttal, he said, "You know, my Daddy makes so much money every Sunday that it takes four grown men to carry it all to him."

Sometimes children do like to brag about their parents. As much as they like to put on airs, however, what children treasure more than anything else is closeness with their parents. A twelve-year-old boy, the son of a missionary in Africa, was sent by his parents to school in the United States. His parents wanted to provide him with every opportunity to have a good education and were willing to endure family separation in order to do what they thought was best for their son. When Christmas came, the parents were in Africa and their son was in school in the United States. Most of the boy's classmates at the boarding school went home for the holidays, but there was no way that he could go home. It was too far and too costly. As he sat in his room, lonely, his housemother happened to walk by. She noticed his loneliness and tried to show him some kindness. She sat down with him on his bed and spoke to him about general things. Then she asked him what he wanted for Christmas. She expected to hear the usual list of things like toys and clothes and money. But the boy surprised her. He stepped over to his dresser, took a picture of his Mom and Dad into his hands and softly said, "I wish My Mom and Dad could step out of this picture and be here with me right now; that's what I want for Christmas." Touched by his sadness, the two of them cried together.

When we confess our faith in our Savior Jesus Christ, it's a kind of boasting we do about him. To confess means to declare the wonderful deeds of him who called us out of darkness into his marvelous light. To confess means to give witness to all the great things that Jesus has done for us and still keeps on doing. There is much that we can brag about when we talk about Jesus, but the most wonderful boast of all is his *closeness* to us, and because of him, God's closeness to us.

At the beginning of his Gospel, St. John confessed his faith in Jesus. He boasted about his God and Savior. John had much to say about the Lord. Jesus the Savior is God, he declares. "In the beginning was the *Word* and the Word was *with* God and the Word *was* God." He is eternal, John tells us, without beginning and without end. Everything was made by him so that not even one single thing came into existence without him. In him was life and light. Like a light shining brilliantly in a dark place, he came shining into the darkness of life, the darkness of sin, death and hell, the darkness of all that is evil. He conquered all the darkness, for the darkness had no power over his light. John confessed the Kingdom, power and the glory of our Savior. But then, saving the very best for last, he confessed the Savior's closeness. "The Word became flesh and dwelt among us," John wrote.

For Luther, this was the chief miracle of Christmas and it is for us as well. God became human and came to be one with us. "His name shall be called Emmanuel, which means 'God with us,'" the angel told Joseph. This is the good news of the season. "To us a Child is born, to us a Son is given." The most important words in that Scripture are the words "to us." For us, to be with us, God came in the flesh. In his beautiful hymn, "From Heaven Above To Earth I Come," Luther gave lyrical confession to this great miracle. He wrote, "Ah Lord, who has created all, how weak art thou, how poor and small . . . Who is this Child, so young and fair? The Blessed Christ Child lieth there . . . Thou com'st to share my misery; what thanks shall I return to thee?"

If it had not been for the birth of Jesus, we would never sing another song we like so well: "What A Friend We Have In Jesus!" If Jesus had not been born, if God had not come in the flesh, there would be no great Friend for us. God would still be a fearsome power, far above us, out of sight, out of touch and frightening. But in Christ Jesus, God is *with* us, *close* to us, *one* with us, a Friend.

There is a fine old film that makes an appearance on the late show just about every Christmas. The film is entitled "Miracle of 42nd Street." It's the story of how good old St. Nick made a little girl's Christmas wishes all come true. The story is charming enough, but there is a problem with it: it shows how little we expect from Christmas. All that people want from Christmas is for their wishes to be granted. We are satisfied with the "miracles" of "peace on earth," of friendship, of gifts and all the other "stuff" of Christmas. In the process, the true miracle of Christmas doesn't do anything for us. What Christmas is really all about is that God in Christ Jesus is *with* us.

Jesus is one with us in every experience of life, from birth to death. We have not a Savior who is unable to sympathize with us in our weaknesses, Scripture tells us, but one who in every respect has experienced all of life, even being tempted to sin as we are, yet without sinning. (Hebrews 4:14) Jesus is one with us. He knows all about life: hunger, thirst, exhaustion, loneliness, rejection, pain, grief, sorrow, sadness, joy. He knows all about life because he lived it for about thirty years. Not only did he experience it, however; he *transformed* it. "I came that you might have life," he said, "and that you might have it more abundantly." He also died, not just to go through it, but through his own death to conquer death and bring life and immortality to light through the Gospel.

St. Paul liked to brag about Jesus as much as did St. John. "If I must boast," Paul wrote, "I will boast of the Lord." Listen to St. Paul's witness about the Babe of Bethlehem, "He is the image of the invisible God, the first-born of all creation; for in him all things were created in heaven and on earth, visible and invisible, whether thrones for dominions or principalities or authorities — all things were created through him and for him. He is before all things and in him all things hold together . . . For in him all the fulness of God was pleased to dwell." (Colossians 1:15-19) As wonderful as all those things are, however, for Paul, as for John, what counted most of all was that Jesus is God with us. And so he also made the confession, "When the time had fully come, God sent forth his Son, born of a woman, born under the law, to redeem all those who were under the law, so that we might receive adoption as sons (heirs) of God." (Galatians 4:4-5) For Paul, what really mattered was that, *because* of Jesus, *in* Christ Jesus, nothing can ever separate us from the love of God. (Romans 8:39)

God with us! "The Word became flesh and dwelt among us." This is the true wonder of Christmas. Sadly, however, John tells us the world does not know this good news; the world does not know him. He came; he is here; but the world does not receive him. What John wrote so long ago we see to be true in the way most people celebrate Christmas: they rejoice in everything *but* Jesus Christ. Sometimes one gets the feeling that Christmas is still a pagan holiday.

December 25th used to be a pagan holiday, you know. This is the date of the Roman Saturnalia, a bawdy celebration of the return of the sun. To "Christianize" this date and to remove the pagan customs, Pope Liberius, in the year 354, declared this day the birthday of our Lord. Many of the customs we still practice were borrowed from pagan sources: giving and receiving presents, evergreens, holly, ivy, mistletoe . . . These things were pagan first and then given Christian significance. One gets the feeling that paganism has reclaimed them. We need to Christianize Christmas all over again.

The world may not know Jesus and the world may not receive him. But to all who do receive him, to all who do believe in him, to you and to me, Jesus gives power to become the children of God, born of God. All who believe in him who is "God with us" he makes to be one with God. Jesus prayed, for us, "As you, Father, are in me and I am in you, let those who believe in me be in us . . ." (John 17:20-21)

And so we are. God is in us and we are in God because of the greatest-ever wonder, the chief miracle of Christmas: That the eternal God was clothed in flesh and blood. Amen

Christmas 1
Luke 2:25-40

Memories

Hidden away in just about every family's photo album is a cute little picture of a baby's buns. Along with all the other photos of baby's first haircut, first birthday, first bike ride, and the like, there's also that one picture, that infamous photo showing off baby's buns. Parents love to have at least one such photo; but the individual whose anatomy is so displayed grows up living in fearful dread that one day his girlfriend or her boyfriend will actually see that awful picture.

It's fun to look through a box of old pictures and to relive all those memories. There's a picture of Mom and Dad when they were first married. There are pictures showing how much more hair Dad had back then, and how dark it was. A picture of your first home. Baby coming home from the hospital. Christmas at Grandpa's farm. Your first high school picture. (Why do people snicker when they see *that* one?) All *kinds* of pictures. We look back and relive our own childhood, or when our children were babies, and we remember special times, special places and special people.

The second chapter of the Gospel of Luke is a lot like a photo album of our Lord's childhood, a glimpse back into the simpler times of his life. Obviously there are no photos for us to look at, but in this chapter we hear a little about our Lord's early life, from his birth through an event in his twelfth year. Not much is told about those years. It's almost as though a whole box of memories was lost.

The memories belong to Mary, the mother of our Lord. She told them to others. They were remembered, and Luke, inspired by

God, wrote them down for us. These memories are not your average memories. There is no recollection here of birthday parties, of first words spoken, of little friends. There is, rather, a testimony to one life that, from its very beginning was God's greatest gift. It is the life of one man who was, from his birth on — and still remains — the Savior of the world.

Looking back into our Lord's childhood we see, first of all, parents who were God-fearing and religious. Mary and Joseph were Jews who believed in God and practiced the religion of the Old Testament. In keeping with Old Testament laws they brought Jesus to the Temple when he was about forty days old, in order to offer there a sacrifice that God prescribed for a new mother and her new child. Luke tells us that Mary "found favor with God." We can only assume that Joseph did too. They found favor with God because God was a vibrant part of their life, and they believed in him, obeyed him and lived in him. Jesus was fortunate to have been blessed with good, God-fearing parents.

Something happened that day when the parents of our Lord carried him, tiny and vulnerable, into the Temple. An old man and an old woman became part of his childhood memories. Simeon and Anna were their names and they feared God also. They were looking for the "consolation of Israel," hoping for God's Messiah, the promised Savior to come. The moment they saw the baby Jesus they recognized him to be the Lord's Christ and spoke of him to all "who were looking for the redemption of Jerusalem." Simeon especially was filled with joy and blessed God for his great gift.

Simeon had been waiting to die. He was an old man who had lived a full life and was ready to go home. The only thing missing was seeing God's salvation, and God had promised him that he would not die until he saw the Savior. God kept his promise to that old man. Simeon saw Jesus. When he saw him, it was the very climax of his life. "Lord, now lettest thou thy servant depart in peace . . . " Simeon prayed. Let me die, Lord, because you have done everything for me that you said you were going to do. Simeon was full of trust in God.

After he prayed his joyful prayer of thanks to God, Simeon then turned his attention to Mary, the Lord's mother. His words to her were not about how cute the baby was, but about the ministry her son would perform. Simeon told Mary that Jesus would be the cause of many falling and rising. All those who rejected Jesus, believing in their own righteousness, were going to be lost, falling to the depths of hell. All those who despaired of themselves because of their sinfulness and looked to Jesus alone for forgiveness and rescue would be saved, lifted up to heaven itself. Then Simeon gave Mary a hint about our Lord's ultimate purpose for coming: his death on the cross in payment for the sins of the world. "A sword will pierce through your own soul also," he told her.

Those words themselves must have caused Mary's heart to skip a beat the moment she heard them. Her baby, this perfect little boy whom she had borne, was going to be a cause of grief for her. She couldn't see how it was possible, but the words surely came back to her the day she stood at the foot of her son's cross and watched him die; the day he gave her to John and she heard him say to her, "Mother, there is your new son."

There's a beautiful new song entitled, "For When Jesus Gets Back Home." In the song a woman sings about how hard it is to know what Mary must have felt all those years that she was with Jesus. Who could know what emotions churned inside her that day in the Temple when Simeon spoke to her and at the Temple again, twelve years later, when she found Jesus after he had been lost? How can we feel what it was like to be the mother of the Lord on that day when Jesus was too busy to see her? Who could know what it felt like when she stood by the cross? In the song, we are told that, above all else Mary felt, she believed that Jesus was her Savior. She believed in his Resurrection. She watched him die and then hurried back home again, we hear in the song, to get things ready for "when Jesus got back home."

All these memories St. Luke recorded for us quite a while after the Lord died, rose again and ascended into heaven. One gets the distinct impression reading them that Mary looked back over our Lord's whole life and saw how, from the very beginning, he came to be the Savior, to give joy to an old man, comfort to an old woman, forgiveness of sins, life and salvation to all who believe in him. He came to live a single, solitary, purposeful life, a life of redemption.

One other figure is prominent in our Lord's "scrapbook": The Holy Spirit. It was through the Holy Spirit that Simeon and Anna knew Jesus. It is through the Holy Spirit that anyone ever knows him. The Gospel of Luke, like his second book, Acts, is a testimony to the work of the Holy Spirit who guides us into the way of peace. He guides us to know Jesus.

People believed in Jesus only because of the Holy Spirit. Isaiah's words apply to Jesus: There was nothing in him that appeared unusual. "He had no form of comeliness that we should look at him, no beauty that we should desire him." (Isaiah 53:2) Even when Jesus did his miracles and shared his majestic teachings, the people weren't impressed. "He's just the son of Joseph the carpenter and Mary his wife," they said. There was no halo around the Lord's head when he ministered in Palestine, no way to tell, just from looking at him, that he was the Christ. The Holy Spirit persuaded the people to believe in him.

The Holy Spirit persuaded Simeon. Luke tells us the Holy Spirit was upon him. One day in the Temple Simeon saw a couple with a new baby. They were not at all unusual. Yet Simeon took that child into his arms and confessed him to be the Christ.

We aren't always able to discern the work of the Holy Spirit in our lives. Sometimes we can't tell he's been with us until we look back and see his work in retrospect. Simeon probably thought he went to the Temple that day just because he had felt like going. He hadn't had much else to do, so he just went by the Temple to see "what was cooking" there. But once he got there he learned the Holy Spirit had guided him to be where the Christ was going to be.

The Holy Spirit is active in our lives, working through God's marvelous coincidences, seeing to it that you and I are at the right place, at the right time, to meet the right people. The Spirit works in us most of all to bring us to meet Jesus, the Christ, our Savior. It's good to be able to look back over our lives and see God's hand in it all, the Holy Spirit guiding us.

The collection of memories about our Lord's childhood ends with these words: "He grew up and became strong, filled with wisdom; (he was very close to God) and the favor of God was upon him." The favor of God was upon Jesus and through Jesus, God's favor is upon each of us. Amen

Christmas 2
John 1:1-18

No Longer Afraid

It's amazingly easy to make people feel guilty and afraid. Say to a child, "Dad wants to talk to you about something!" and immediately a worried look will come across the child's face as he begins to comb through his memory for something he may have done wrong. The same thing happens when a student is told, "You have to go to the principal's office." When an adult hears, "The boss wants you in his office right now!" rarely do we anticipate a bonus or a pat on the back. Instead, the first thought that crosses our minds usually is a question: "What did I do *this* time?"

People tend naturally to feel guilty. Whether we have actually done anything to be guilty of or not doesn't matter all that much. Our predisposition to guilt is the result of our imperfection, our sin. We know that we aren't perfect, we aren't all that we should be even when we are doing our best. So it's easy to feel guilty and afraid.

Even more frightening than having to talk to Dad, the principal or the boss, is having to stand before God. God is perfect and he has said to us, "You must be perfect as your heavenly Father is perfect." (Matthew 5:48) We know we can't be perfect; we can't be what God wants us to be and, because of it, the thought of speaking to him or seeing him is frightening. Even some people who say they are Christian are still frightened enough about God that they will say they aren't sure that he will "let them into heaven" when they die. It's easy to be afraid of God.

The children of Israel were scared out of their wits when God spoke to them at Mount Sinai. God came to the mountain with power and glory. Lightning flashed; thunder rolled; smoke poured off the mountain. God was there. The people saw it and quivered in fear. "You talk to God for us," they said to Moses, "only don't let him talk to us or else we will surely die." (Exodus 20:19)

Not only God, but anything perfect, anything coming from God, frightens people. Angels came from God to bring messages to people. Each time they came, the first words they had to speak were always, "Do not be afraid." Zacharias, the father of John the Baptizer, was afraid when he saw the angel; so were Joseph, Mary, and the shepherds. None expected to hear good news. Apparently, they all thought they were in trouble. Confronted with the perfect holiness of God, they were overwhelmed by their imperfection and sin — and they were afraid.

But the angels did not bring *any* of them bad news! They brought *good* news. "Good news of a great joy which will come to all people; for to you is born this day in the city of David a Savior who is Christ the Lord." (Luke 2:10-11) The angels brought good news about the birth of One who came to take our guilt away; One who came to remove our fear and give us joy and confidence in its place; One named Jesus who came to be perfect for us, in our place, that we might be perfect in him.

As frightened as people were by angels and as afraid as they were of God, there may not have been anyone who was ever afraid of Jesus except for the single exception of the moneychangers whom he cast out of the Temple. Children came running up to him for blessing. They knew they wouldn't be turned away. Tax collectors, prostitutes, a crucified thief, all kinds of people with lots of reasons to feel guilty and afraid, came to Jesus. "I don't condemn you . . . ," he said to the woman taken in adultery. A preacher might well have made such people feel very ashamed; but Jesus made them feel wonderful. They knew that he accepted them, loved them and forgave them.

Jesus did all that even though he, too, was perfect — or, perhaps more accurately, *because* he was perfect. Everything about us that is lacking and empty before God, was abundantly full in Christ Jesus. Where we are imperfect, he was perfect. Where we sin, he never sinned. "From his fulness," John tells us, "we receive grace upon grace." Jesus was perfect for us, in our place. Because of him God counts us perfect also.

St. John tells us that no one would ever have known God except for the fact that Jesus made him known. The way that Jesus was to the people — accepting, forgiving, kind and loving — is how God really is. "The Lord is merciful and gracious, slow to anger and abounding in steadfast love," Scripture tells us. (Psalm 103) He forgives all our iniquities. Precisely because God is this way, he sent Jesus to be our Savior. He sent Jesus to be God with us, accepting, forgiving and life-giving. He sent Jesus to be perfect and to make us perfect so that we might be one with him, our perfect God. Not only can we now be unafraid of him, but we can now be close to him as well.

Because of Jesus, all of God's children can exchange a message of guilt and fear for this message instead: "Let us then with confidence draw near to the throne of grace, that we may receive mercy and find grace to help in time of need." (Hebrews 4:16) "Through him [Jesus] we have confidence in God . . . " (1 Peter 1:21) We know that God is not only God but he is our Father and Christ our Savior.

We know this because even though we cannot, in and of ourselves, do all that we have to do, Jesus has done it all for us. He does not tell us all that *we* have to do, but rather shares with us all that *he* has done *for us*. He lived, died and rose again, and that is enough. It is perfect. When we ask in fear and guilt, "What do I have to do to be saved? How can I make God like me so I don't have to be afraid of him?" Jesus answers, "You don't have to do *anything*. Just believe in me and live in me; I have done it all for you."

God wants to see you one of these days. We know that one of these days we will have to stand before God and listen to him. That could make us afraid, but it really doesn't have to. We stand before him every moment of our life and are judged against his holiness and perfection. There is no reason for us to be afraid now or later because we know that what God says to us is only what he said to his perfect Son. Because of Jesus, he says to you and to me also, "This is my beloved child, my son, my daughter, with whom I am well pleased."

That promise strengthens us, in Jesus' name. Amen

The Epiphany of Our Lord
Matthew 2:1-12

Just Follow The Signs

"God so loved the world . . . " begins one of our best-known Scripture verses. God loved the world! He didn't love only one small corner of the world. He didn't love only one little race, one tiny tribe in the world. God loved the world! He loved Jews and Gentiles alike. He loved a man and a woman named Joseph and Mary. He loved some shepherds. He loved some Wise Men living way off in the East someplace, nobody knows exactly where. God loved the world, even nasty, murderous, old King Herod, who tried to kill his only-begotten, just-born Son. "God so loved the world that he gave his only-begotten Son that whoever believes in him should not perish but have eternal life." (John 3:16) God loved you and me.

God's love for the world expresses itself chiefly in his strong desire for the salvation of the world. Because God loved the world he sent his Son to be the Savior of the world. "God wants all people to be saved and to come to know the truth," St. Paul wrote. (1 Timothy 2:4) To that end, God is active in our lives, in all people's lives, in a personal, intimate and individual way.

God has a number of ways of working in our lives. One way in which he is active is through wonderful signs that he gives us to draw us to himself. Some signs are more majestic than others. Some signs are very hard to see, to be aware of. But in each life there are signs — signs that, when followed, lead to the only true God and Jesus Christ whom he sent. "The grace of God that brings salvation," Paul wrote, "has appeared to all people . . . " (Titus 2:11) One way that grace appears is through signs.

Look at the sign that God worked in the lives of the Wise Men: The Star! When the Lord Jesus was born, God announced the birth of his Son with a once-in-forever Star in the Sky. God didn't send out cute little hospital cards with a picture of a wrinkled-prune-looking baby on it. God put a brilliant Star in the sky to announce the birth of his Son. Nobody knows what star this was. Many have speculated about it, some thinking it was a constellation of some sort. It would have been great to be able to see it. It was a special Star that God created to announce the most wonderful news ever: the birth of his only Son, the Savior of the world. It was a Star that God brought into being for the specific purpose of bringing the Wise Men to know him. It may well have been a Star that will never again be seen.

The Star was not the only sign given in our text, however. The Star was the sign God gave to the Wise Men. The Wise Men were the sign God gave to King Herod. Think about it: When these strangers dropped in from nowhere asking Herod about the new King of the Jews, that must have gotten Herod's attention much as the Star got the Wise Men's attention. When the Wise Men came to Herod asking about Jesus, that was God's action in Herod's life calling him to come worship the Savior also. The Wise Men really did not have to ask Herod where Jesus was. The Star had already brought them so close to the Lord that, had they followed it a little farther, it would have led them right to Jesus. It was there, right over the house where Jesus was! The Wise Men went out of their way to get to the palace. Their detour was God's way of getting the word about Jesus to Herod. It was God's sign in Herod's life.

Just as the Wise Men were a sign to Herod, Herod, in turn, became a sign to the chief priests and the scribes. When the Wise Men asked the King, "Where is he who has been born King of the Jews?" Herod didn't know the answer. He turned the question over to the priests and the scribes. These men were actually given two signs by God: Herod was the first; the record of the Holy Scriptures was the second.

Here, then, were three separate signs from God, each given because of his love, because of his desire to save all people. God loved the Wise Men, and Herod, and the priests and the scribes. He wanted to save them all. To that end, he gave signs in their lives to lead them to the Savior. God was faithful, but the people were not always so. Each sign was greeted with a different reaction.

The Wise Men (good for them!) followed the sign of the Star. They saw the Star in the East and immediately answered its call. They searched for the newborn King. They wanted to worship him, to bring him gifts. Their search ended when they knelt, in exceedingly great joy, before the Baby Jesus and adored him. The Star, God's sign for them, had led them to their salvation.

Herod (shame on him) responded to God's sign in his life negatively. Instead of going with the Wise Men to worship Jesus, he made plans to kill his Savior. Our text tells us that Herod was bothered by the news of a new King. Herod didn't understand who Jesus was at all. He thought the Baby was a threat to his throne. Herod was a wicked man. No matter how hard God tried to reach him, how clear a sign God gave him, he refused to follow, choosing instead to reject God and to die in his sins.

Saddest of all were the priests and the scribes. They understood all about the sign. They knew what the sign meant. They quoted God's prophets in their response to Herod. They knew all the facts. But they did not go to worship Jesus. They understood, but they did not believe. This is the only thing that could be worse than regarding God a "bother" the way Herod did. Seeing his action in our life, understanding his work, but *not doing anything about it,* neither worshiping him nor believing in him nor rejecting him — that's a colossal tragedy. Many people treat God just this way, however. They simply ignore him.

Perhaps we could try to defend Herod and the priests by saying that they didn't have the same chance the Wise Men had. The signs given to them were not as impressive as the sign given to the Wise Men. Maybe if they had seen a Star they would have followed it also. After all, bigger and better signs make for bigger and better reactions, right? Not necessarily. Besides, who says they didn't see the Star? The problem was not with their *sign;* the problem was with their *reaction.*

One gets the impression from reading this story that the Wise Men were the only ones who ever saw the Star. Nobody else came running to find out what it was all about, did they? The Gospels don't tell us about a mob scene suddenly developing at the stable. Only the Wise Men came. Yet, if the Star was all that fantastic, as it certainly must have been, then surely other people saw it also, wouldn't you think? Why didn't they come running too? Because there's a problem with the signs God gives to people. Most of the time people don't notice them, or, if they notice, they don't pay any attention. People tend to ignore the signs God gives.

Our Lord Jesus lamented, concerning many of the people of his day, that they could interpret the appearance of the sky, forecasting the weather by the color of the clouds, *yet they could not interpret the signs of the times.* They could see tomorrow's weather, but they couldn't see the Savior standing in their midst today. (Matthew 16:3) The problem is that people rarely, if ever, stop to ask, "What is God trying to *say* to me?" Things happen around us and to us and we go on blissfully unaware of God, acting as if he has nothing to do with what is going on.

It's sad to see this happen. God reaches out to people. He's active in their lives in some special way. But all he ever becomes to them is what he was to Herod: a bother.

I'm thinking of a family I know. They are not members of this church. While they say they believe in God, they never worship him publicly. There is no visible evidence in their lives of faith. God has done many things for them, giving them many signs in their lives by filling their lives with wonderful things, but his call to them to live for him appears to be too much of a bother. We read in the Bible, "Don't you know that the kindness of God is meant to lead you to repentance?" (Romans 2:4) We need to pray more for them.

God's signs are all around us: in nature, like the Wise Men's Star; and in people, the way he used the Wise Men as a sign to Herod. There is always the sign of his holy Word, the same sign he gave to the priests. Some of God's signs are even a little spooky. For example — when a person is scheduled for a certain flight, misses the plane and learns later that the plane crashed. Do you think God might be trying to say something to that person?

The prophets of the Old Testament believed that all the politics of their day were signs from God and they tried to use those signs to call God's people to repentance. Might the politics of our nation, the affairs of our world, be a sign from God calling us to repentance also? We need to ask ourselves regularly, "What is God trying to tell me?" because in his mercy, God is active in our lives, trying to tell us how much he loves us and how dearly he wants our salvation.

Thank God that in his grace he has made us alert to his signs in our life. We have seen God's signs, signs that all Christians share, like Baptism, the Word and the Body and Blood of Jesus, and individual signs that belong to each of us uniquely. Through the Spirit we see the signs and follow them to Jesus, the Savior. We see the signs, we believe and are saved.

"Just follow the signs," people say when giving directions. Those are our directions for the Epiphany season ahead of us. That's all we really have to do. Follow the signs God gives us, signs that lead to the Savior as surely as the star led the Wise Men to Bethlehem. Signs that lead us into life. Amen

The Baptism of Our Lord
Mark 1:4-11

A God Pleasing Savior and God Pleasing People

One of the basic rules of interpersonal relationships is that you can please some of the people some of the time, but you can never please all the people all the time. There is a children's story that illustrates how totally useless it is even to try always to please everyone. The story tells about a father, his son and their donkey. As their journey began, the father led the donkey and the boy rode. But because some people criticized the boy for being lazy, he got down from the donkey and let his father ride. But because some other people criticized the father for not caring about his son, the father got down and walked next to his son. But because some other people laughed at them for having a donkey and not riding it, they both began to ride. And when some people condemned them for overburdening the poor donkey, together the father and his son carried the animal into town.

No matter how hard we try, we can always find someone who will not be pleased with what we do. Mom fixes Dad's favorite dinner and the kids hate it. Dad builds a tree house which the kids love and Mom hates it. A person makes a decision to please himself or herself and everybody gets angry at him because of it.

A good deal of the frustration we feel much of the time is the direct result of our inability to please people. We want to make people happy, to be true to ourselves while, at the same time, being what others want us to be. We want to be good persons, good friends, husbands, wives, fathers, and children; to live up to people's expectations of us. Often, all we get from trying, however, is a feeling of futility and hopelessness. Just to save our sanity we finally have to make up our minds to please some and displease others. And we hope, in so doing, that we pick the right people for each.

If we lived in a perfect world and were all perfect people, this would never be a problem. But because we are imperfect, because we are sinful, we are unable perfectly to please one another and to be pleased. People expect too much from other people; people don't give as much as they expect to get. This imbalance is affirmation of sin, for it causes separation in our lives. Our Lord Jesus was perfect, but he couldn't please all the imperfect people around him; so they killed him.

For the Christian, this problem is compounded because there is one more person to please. Actually, it's a great deal more than a person; it's God. In addition to all the other demands that are placed on us, Christians also want to please God. In response to God's love for us, moved by his great kindness and mercy, touched by his redeeming grace, we want with all our heart to obey God and live for him as Jesus lived and died and rose again for us. But this, also, is something that often produces nothing more than frustration, for we know that we sin and that our sins do not please God. Because of our sins, because we fail to please God, we are filled with hurt, remorse and grief. St. Paul himself wrestled with this dilemma and confessed, in near despair, "I do not do the good I want but the evil I do not want is what I do." (Romans 7)

Is it possible to please God? Yes, but not by virtue of anything that we do. We can please God only because of what God has done for us and in us. Christians know that, in spite of all our sins, God is still pleased with us because of all that Jesus Christ has done for us. Christians know and believe that they cannot please God by themselves because they are sinful. Christians begin to please God the moment they confess their sins, their total inadequacy, and confess their faith in Jesus Christ the Savior. God is pleased with all who believe in his Son. Not because of what they have done but because of what Jesus has done for them. Christians go on to please God more and more throughout their lives because of what the Holy Spirit keeps on doing in them.

I used to work for a man who said he believed in God but didn't believe in Jesus. He was a very successful man, having built from nearly nothing a company that was worth several million dollars. He was very proud of what he had accomplished and convinced that he could take care of himself in every way. He didn't like the idea that he could not make himself good enough for God. In one of our many talks about religion he said, "If I have to believe in Jesus to make it into heaven, I guess I just won't make it!" This is the difference between Christians and unbelievers. Christians accept the fact that they can please God only through Jesus Christ. Unbelievers try to please God on their own merits. In the process, just like the Pharisees of old, they reject the purpose of God for themselves.

Our Lord Jesus was subject to all the pressures to please people that we feel. People expected all kinds of things from him. They wanted him to be a miracle worker, a healer, someone to feed them, most of all a warrior king who would make their lives easy. And God wanted him to be the Savior of the world, to live a perfect, sinless life, die an innocent and obedient death and come back to life again to conquer death once and for all. Jesus didn't live up to all the expectations about him. He only lived up to what God expected. Ultimately, that's all *we* have to live up to.

What God expected from Jesus was that he would be the Savior of the world. God expected Jesus to do nothing for his own sake but to give up his whole life as a ransom for the world, to pay for the world's sins. Everything that Jesus did, from the moment he emptied himself, took the form of a servant, and was born in human likeness (Philippians 2:8), he did always and only so that God would be pleased with us. Jesus lived, not for his own sake, but for ours, that he might share with us in all our experiences. Jesus died, not to pay for his own sins, but so that through his suffering we might be forgiven. Jesus came back to life again not for himself, but for us, so that we might be free from death and have eternal life in him.

In everything, Jesus did it all for us. Even his Baptism he did for us. Jesus was baptized not because he needed to be made perfect but because we needed that. Jesus had no sin, nothing to repent of and be forgiven for. He was holy. We *do* have sin; we *do* need to repent and to be forgiven. So that forgiveness might be ours, Jesus was baptized.

When Jesus came to John to be baptized by him, John couldn't understand what in the world was going on. "I need to be baptized by *you*," he said to Jesus. John knew and confessed that Jesus was mightier than he. John tried to stop Jesus. But the Savior said to him, "Let's do it this way for now in order to fulfill all righteousness." (Matthew 3:15) Let's do it this way, Jesus said, so that I can accomplish all that you can't do for God to be pleased with you. And John baptized him. Then the heavens were opened, Mark tells us, the Holy Spirit appeared, and God said, "This is my beloved Son with whom I am well pleased." The heavens were opened for us and what God said to our Savior, he really said to all of us who believe in his Son. Because of Jesus, God is pleased with us.

What that means for us in our daily lives is that we don't have to worry about pleasing God anymore. There will always be people who will be displeased with us, but God will always be pleased with us because of all that Jesus has done for us. This does not mean that we can do anything we want to do. Our sins will always hurt God and it pleases him when we are sorry for them also, and when we hurt over them as he does. What it *does* mean is that God will live in us and that his Holy Spirit who was present at our Lord's Baptism in the form of a dove will be present in our lives also. The Holy Spirit will teach us to deny ungodliness and worldly lusts and will empower us to live holy and God-pleasing lives. Knowing that God is pleased with us is good news that sets us free to want to please God because Jesus lives in us, not because we "have to."

You can please some of the people some of the time and all of the people none of the time. In Christ Jesus we can please God all the time because of all that our Savior has done for us and because of what the Holy Spirit keeps on doing in us. In Jesus' name. Amen

Epiphany 2
John 1:43-51

Jesus Knows Everything!
Jesus Is God!

It is part of God's nature to know all things. We call this quality *omniscience*. God knows everything. There is nothing he does not know. Jesus once said that the Father's knowledge is so total that he even knows when a single bird falls out of the sky and he knows the number of hairs we have on our head. In the case of some of us it is easier for him to keep track of that last statistic.

That God knows how much hair we have is just one indication of how intimately he knows each one of us. In Hebrews we read that "no creature is hidden to him but all are open and laid bare to his eyes." (Hebrews 4:13) Job confessed that "God's eyes are upon the ways of a man and he sees all his steps." (Job 31:21) God's knowledge of us is so perfect, Jesus said in the Sermon on the Mount, that he knows all our needs even before we ask him. (Matthew 6:8)

King David was very much aware of how personally and completely God knew him. He confessed, "O Lord, you have examined me and you know me. You know everything I do; from far away you understand all my thoughts. You see me, whether I am working or resting, when I rise up and when I sit down. You know all my actions. Even before I speak you already know what I will say . . . Your knowledge of me is overwhelming; it is too deep for me to understand." God knows all things.

Today's Gospel lesson informs us that Jesus knows all things also. He knew all about Nathanael even though they had never met.

As Nathanael walked toward the Lord for the first time, Jesus could already say about him that he was an Israelite indeed, in whom was no guile. Nathanael looked back at Jesus and asked in wonder, "How do you know me?"

When Nathanael first heard about Jesus from Philip he was not impressed at all. "Can anything good come out of Nazareth?" he asked. Nazareth was a little hick town and Nathanael figured all you get out of a hick town is hick people. But when he met the Lord face to face and saw how well Jesus already knew him, he confessed, "Rabbi, you are the Son of God! You are the King of Israel!"

Our Gospel lesson manifests Jesus Christ to us as true God because Jesus knows all things also, just as God does. In Hebrews we read that Jesus "reflects the glory of God and bears the very stamp of his nature." (Hebrews 1:3) Just as it is part of God's nature to know everything, so it is also part of our Lord's nature. Jesus knows everything. Jesus is God.

Nathanael is not the only one who was ever impressed by the knowledge of Jesus. That happened for the first time, St. Luke tells us, when Jesus was only twelve years old. Together with his parents, he went up to Jerusalem for the Feast of the Passover. They stayed several days. When the Feast was over, the parents of our Lord started for home, supposing that Jesus was in the crowd of travelers with them. But he wasn't; he was in the Temple, sitting among the teachers, listening to them and asking them questions. St. Luke tells us that "all who heard him were amazed at his understanding and his answers." (Luke 2:47)

Jesus knows everything. Jesus is God. One day Jesus was in Samaria. He was thirsty so he sat down by a well and waited to get a drink. He didn't have anything with which to draw water so he had to wait for somebody who could help him to come by. Presently a woman of the area came to the well. She was the real reason why Jesus was there. They began to speak. Jesus asked her some questions about her personal life but the questions were asked in such a way that she could tell that he already knew the answers. Because of his intimate knowledge of her, she believed in him and confessed to her neighbors, "He told me all that I ever did." (John 4:39)

The Pharisees were regularly frustrated in their confrontations with Jesus because he always knew what they were thinking. "Jesus knew their thoughts," Matthew tells us; "he perceived their wickedness." (Matthew 12:25, 22:18) "Jesus knew all people and needed no one to tell him about man for he himself knew what was in man, "St. John confessed. (John 2:25) He even knew that one of his disciples would betray him, from the moment he was chosen to be a disciple. All the disciples, in the last few hours before our Lord's death, confessed, "Now we know that you know all things . . . (and) by this we believe that you came from God." (John 16:20)

Jesus knows everything. Jesus is God. Jesus knows us. "I know my own and my own know me," he said. (John 10:14) This is God's seal of approval on us, for the sake of Jesus Christ. "The Lord knows all those who are his." (2 Timothy 2:19) St. Paul testified, "If any one love God, the same is known of him." (1 Corinthians 8:3) Jesus knows us, everything about us, our strengths and weaknesses, our joys and our sorrows, our successes and our failures, our sins and our victories over sin. He knows everything.

The fact that Jesus knows everything about us can be either good news or bad news. We decide which it is. It is good news if we look at his omniscience and believe that because he knows everything about us he takes care of us, providing all our needs even before we ask him. It is bad news if we try to hide from him. Adam and Eve decided it was bad news, after they sinned. They knew that God knew what they had done. They decided to be afraid of God and run away from him. They tried to hide from him because of what they had done. It would have worked, except for the fact that our all-knowing God knew where they were.

Like Adam and Eve, many people still choose to pretend that God does not know everything. They try to hide things from him. The Pharisees of our Lord's day believed they could hide their wickedness from God and they hated Jesus, because he showed them over and over again that there was no hiding place. Like the Pharisees, people who try to hide from God today invariably wind up hating him also because he always finds them.

Little children try to hide from their parents. They try to conceal facts from Mom and Dad, but "the old man" and "the old lady" know what's going on. My children are always amazed that I know what they are doing. I tell them it's because fathers know everything. They don't believe that as much as they used to anymore. Even more than parents, God knows everything.

Better than to try to hide from our all-knowing God and Savior is to expose ourselves to him, to confess what he already knows about us anyway. To confess means, in its most basic sense, to expose oneself. The tax collector Jesus told about in one of his parables knew that God knew all about his sin and it was senseless to try and hide. So he confessed, "O God, have mercy on me, a sinner." God accepted him, Jesus tells us in his story, and forgave him and he was justified.

The good news about our Lord Jesus Christ is not only that he knows all things, but that he accepts us and loves us as we are, in spite of all that he knows about us. Jesus knew all the dirty details about that woman caught in adultery one day. She couldn't hide anything after the people dragged her out in front of him for punishment. He forgave her. Jesus knew all about the public sins of that woman who washed his feet with her tears. She didn't try to hide and he forgave her. He knew all about the weaknesses of Peter and James and John and Judas; still he called them to be his disciples. He knew the record of the thief crucified next to him, a record that could no longer be hidden even though the other criminal still tried to hide it. To the one who exposed himself, who confessed, "Lord, remember me when you come to your Kingdom," Jesus promised, "Today you will be with me in Paradise."

Jesus knows everything. There is no hiding from him. But when we expose ourselves to him, confessing our sins, there is no longer any need to hide, for he takes all our sins away; he forgives us; he accepts us and loves us. Then, knowing that he knows everything about us, there is no threat to us.

Best of all, Jesus knows the way to heaven. He told Nathanael, " . . . you will see heaven opened and the angels of God ascending and descending on the Son of Man." Jesus knows the way to heaven because *he is* the way. "I am the Way," Jesus said. "No one comes to the Father but by me." (John 14:6) All who believe in Jesus, our all-knowing Savior, have eternal life.

There used to be a chilling radio drama many years ago that always began with these words: "Who knows what evil lurks in the hearts of men? The Shadow knows!" The Shadow was a mystical, magical agent of discovery. Somehow he always managed to know who the "bad guys" were and how to get them caught. The Shadow was imaginary. God is real. And God knows everything. Because he is true God, Jesus knows everything also. He knows everything about us, and he loves us in spite of all of it. In Jesus' precious name. Amen

Epiphany 3
Mark 1:14-20

The Best Advertising of All

One of the biggest industries in the United States today is the production of advertising. Billboards, signs on benches, magazines, newspapers, placards on the sides of buses, messages on the insides of match books, "junk" mail, computer phone calls, radio and, of course, television, all seek to commercial-ize us, to sell us something. Commercials make a host of promises. We're told that if we just use what they sell, people will notice us; we'll be healthier, happier, sexier; smell better; look better; feel better; get just about everything we want. I'd hate to add up the amount of time each day that is ruined by commercials. Kids, especially, are fascinated with them and affected by them (most of the time affected badly).

As much advertising as takes place, however, everyone knows that the best form of advertising ever invented and the one that is still most successful is word-of-mouth — people telling other people. About forty years ago there used to be an automobile named the Packard. Packard was the last car manufacturer to get into advertising. It didn't happen until old man Packard died, because whenever he was approached to buy some advertising for his cars he always said, "Don't need any; just ask the man who owns one." After his death, "Ask the man who owns one" became the Packard slogan.

Our Lord Jesus Christ is also known through word-of-mouth advertising. That's how the word about him gets out. Only the Shepherds at the first Christmas heard the good news from angels. Only the Wise Men were led by a Star. Just a comparative few were touched by miracles. Almost everybody came to know Jesus Christ, and is still coming to know him, through word-of-mouth advertising, one person telling another.

The Ethiopian eunuch of Candace is a good example. He was riding home from Jerusalem one day. As he rode along, he was reading the Scriptures, but he couldn't understand what he was reading. God sent Philip to him and Philip spoke to him, telling him all the good news of Jesus. The eunuch believed, was baptized, and saved. It happened through word-of-mouth advertising.

In the case of our Lord Jesus we don't call it advertising. There are other names we use: preaching, witnessing, sharing, testifying, evangelizing. Basically, however, all it is is word-of-mouth advertising, one person telling another. Remember how you came to know Jesus: Somebody told you about him. Maybe it was your mom or your dad, when you were just a child. Maybe it was a friend. Maybe there was more than one person. Somehow, someone told you about the Lord, just as I am doing now, and through that good word, God brought you to faith.

Our Gospel lesson reminds us that John the Baptizer was one of the first to get the word out about Jesus. He appeared in the wilderness, preaching, preparing the way of the Lord, calling people to repent for the Kingdom of God was at hand. John dressed so conspicuously in a coat of camel's hair and ate such weird food — locusts and wild honey — that he was a visual aid all by himself. But the people came, and they listened, and many believed when he pointed at Jesus and announced, "Behold the Lamb of God that takes away the sins of the world."

After John was arrested, our Lord Jesus himself took up the task of getting the word out. He came, preaching the Gospel of God, Mark tells us, and saying, "The time is fulfilled and the Kingdom of God is at hand; repent and believe in the Gospel." The ministry of our Lord Jesus, our Savior, included not only miracles, not just his death and Resurrection, but also his preaching. Matthew even records one of his sermons for us: the Sermon on the Mount.

Sharing the good news of the Kingdom of God, I believe, is what Jesus wanted most of all to do. One time, when his disciples tried to get him to settle down in one place, Jesus said, "Let us go on to the next towns, that I may preach there also; for that is why I came out. and he went throughout all Galilee, preaching . . . " telling the good news. (Mark 1:38-39)

Some of the people who heard that good news were the disciples. They not only heard what Jesus had to say to them, but were called by Jesus to go and tell that good news to others also. Jesus called them to be "fishers of men," to get the word out about the Savior. Their testimony would be the "bait" by which people would be drawn to Jesus and get hooked on him, believe in him. "You shall be my witnesses," Jesus said to them. (Acts 1:8) What you hear from me proclaim to everyone around you, Jesus told them. St. Luke tells us they never stopped telling the good news of Christ our Savior. (Acts 5:42)

Not only the disciples were called to give word-of-mouth advertising about Jesus, but all who believed in him and followed him were called to do so. One such witness was a man out of whom Jesus cast a mob of demons. The Lord was in the country of the Gerasenes. In the area lived a crazy man, a man filled with demons. He lived in the cemetery, ran around naked, was extremely violent, and no one was able to control him. He regularly broke free from chains and any other attempts to bind him. Only from Satan he could not break free. Jesus set him free from his possession, casting the demons out from him. The Savior gave him life such as everybody else had — and eternal life to boot. Out of gratitude so great the man wanted to give his life to Jesus, he begged the Lord for permission to be with him, to go with him. But Jesus told him, "Go home to your friends, and tell them how much the Lord has done for you and how he has had mercy on you." (Mark 5:19) Go tell them, Jesus said.

Through the words of his people, Jesus is revealed; he is manifested to others. It happens through your words and mine, too. Through our words God comes to people and brings them to faith. All we do is tell the good news. God does everything else, but he does it through us, our word-of-mouth advertising.

Word-of-mouth advertising isn't very flashy. A full-scale Dr. Pepper musical is much more impressive. But word-of-mouth works better. Talking about Jesus doesn't seem very impressive either. Miracles, stars and angels get much more attention. Still God uses word-of-mouth, one person telling another, telling the same thing Jesus told: "The Kingdom of God is at hand, repent and believe in the Gospel."

It is apparent that we fail to appreciate the value and the power of the spoken word about Jesus. We're a lot like most of the people who listened to Jesus preach. They didn't care about words; they didn't want to listen; all they wanted were signs, miracles, flashy attention-getters. Jesus condemned them, saying, "Unless you see signs and wonders you will not believe." "An evil and adulterous generation seeks for a sign." (John 4:48; Matthew 12:39) The words Jesus spoke said as much about him as any sign ever could.

In the spoken word about Jesus, no matter which believer in Jesus speaks it, is power — tremendous power. St. Paul wrote "that it pleased God through the folly of what we preach to save all those who believe." (1 Corinthians 1:21-23) God chose, in his wisdom, to bring the good news of salvation to people through something that appears to be foolish and insignificant. It comes through talking about Jesus.

Jesus lived, died and rose again to pay for all our sins and to make us one with God. That's the good news. It becomes *our* good news when someone tells us about it, we hear it and believe. It becomes *someone else's* good news when we tell *them* about it, they hear and believe. "Faith comes from what is heard," Paul wrote, when what is heard is the good news of Jesus Christ. (Romans 10:17) God reveals himself and makes himself known through what we say. What an honor and a privilege!

Because people generally do not do enough word-of-mouth advertising about anything, it has become the thing to do in our time to pay people to talk about a product. It ought not to be that way about Jesus. We have all been called to tell the good news.

Don't say, "It's only words," because it is far more than that. The words count. If you ever have the misfortune of being arrested, you will know just how much your words count when the arresting officer says, in effect, "Be careful what you say because your words can and will be held against you in a court of law." Words have a great deal of power, especially when they are words telling about Jesus. Then, in the words there is the power of God to save all who believe, for in the words God reveals himself to us.

In Jesus' name. Amen

Epiphany 4
Mark 1:21-28

Even The Demons Believe!

Say the word "demon" and the first thing that might pop into your mind is the image of a child you know. Sometimes we describe an ornery child as "a little demon." But in the Bible, the word demon is never used that lightly. It is a word that is always used seriously and fearfully to describe one of the forces of evil, an unclean spirit.

St. Mark records for us the story of one demon who filled a father's life with agony because of the way he possessed the man's son. Shortly after the Transfiguration of our Lord, a man came to Jesus with a pitiful request. "Teacher, I brought my son to you because he has a spirit," the father said. The demon used to seize the boy, dash him to the ground, make him foam at the mouth and grind his teeth. It would cause his body to become rigid all over. At the very moment that the father brought the boy to Jesus, Mark tell us, the demon tormented the boy again, casting him down to the ground right there in the street.

Jesus was filled with pity and compassion. "How long has the boy been like this?" he asked the father. "From infancy," the father replied in desperation, adding, "and often it has cast him into the fire and into the water to destroy him . . . Have pity on us and help us," the man begged. (Mark 9:14-24) Jesus did help them; he cast out the demon.

For that father and for Jesus, demons were all too real and their torment just as real. Demons possessed anybody, adults and children alike, causing blindness, deafness, sometimes symptoms that looked like epilepsy. One girl, out of whom Paul cast a demon, was possessed for the sake of foretelling the future. Because of what the demon did in her, she was enslaved and forced to work for her master's gain. St. Matthew tells us that a mob of demons Jesus cast out of one man went into a herd of swine, causing them all to run off a cliff into the sea and drown.

Demons are hard for us to believe in because of our sophistication. Much of what the Bible writers attributed to demons could easily be explained today in terms of mental and physical illness. We are tempted to dismiss that concerning which they wrote, attributing it to nothing more than ancient superstition. We might find it easy to explain away demons also, except for two things: Jesus believed they were real and the demons knew Jesus before almost anyone else ever did. Knowing Jesus is not something that automatically happens in those who are merely ill.

In our Gospel lesson today, the testimony about the godhood of our Lord Jesus Christ comes from a demon. Jesus was in a synagogue in Capernaum. Suddenly a man possessed by a demon burst into the place, disrupting the worship and confronted our Lord. "What have you to do with us, Jesus of Nazareth?" the demon asked; "Have you come to destroy us? I know who you are, the Holy One of God!" A demon testified about Jesus! A demon knew who Jesus was! A demon called him the Holy One of God!

This was not the only time that a demon gave witness to the divinity of our Lord. Mark tells us that whenever Jesus confronted a demon, "they fell down before him and cried out, 'You are the Son of God'!" (Mark 3:11) Luke tells us the demons knew that Jesus "was the Christ"! (Luke 4:41)

It seems more than a little strange that demons should know Jesus and give witness to him. This kind of testimony could hurt a person more than help. Ever since the Garden of Eden we have known better than to listen to what the devil says, for he is a liar. For this reason, Jesus commanded the demons not to speak about him.

How in the world did they know him? They knew him, not because of who *they* were, but because of who *he* is: True God, the One who has power to destroy them. St. James wrote, "The demons believe — and shudder." (James 2:19) Like that demon in Capernaum that cried out in fear, "Have you come to destroy us?" all demons know that Jesus is the Son of God who was manifested for this very purpose, "that he might destroy the works of the devil." (1 John 3:8)

The deity of our Lord and Savior Jesus is made manifest to us not only by virtue of the fact that the demons recognized him and announced him as the Christ, the Holy One of God. We also know that Jesus is God by virtue of his power over the demons. "With authority he commands even the unclean spirits and they obey him," the people said in amazement after Jesus cast out that demon in Capernaum. It had never happened that way before. They had always been powerless before demons until Jesus came. He cast out all the demons. Not one of them was able to stand up against him. All were defeated — because he is God. Only God has power over demons; Jesus has that power because he is God.

There are demons in our lives that control us as harmfully as demons tormented people in our Lord's day. The demons that run rampant in our lives are things such as pride, guilt, envy, an unforgiving spirit, a favorite sin. Sometimes these things control us so completely that we are powerless against them.

Recently I spoke to a man oppressed by the demon of pride. I'd never met him before but he called to talk to me about a problem he has because of a decision he made. The decision was a bad one and it put him between a rock and a hard place. Deep down in his heart I believe he knows it was a bad decision, but, in his own words, "I've come too far to turn back now." He is going to lose something that means a great deal to him because the demon of pride will not allow him to say, "I was wrong." It will not allow him to change his mind. It is driving him to do something that he really does not want to have to do. Sad, isn't it? Pride, like a demon, causes a great deal of separation in our lives.

Pride combined with envy is a demon that pushes and pushes and pushes people to "keep up with the Joneses." Actually, it never just pushes us to keep up; it always pushes us to do better, get more, have more. Because of this demon, people in families lose touch with each other; they sit in nice, big houses and never talk to each other; they are always too tired for each other; they fall apart.

About a year ago the city of Plano, Texas, experienced the kind of tragedy this demon can cause to happen. Plano lived through the nightmare of multiple suicides. Six young people, aged 14 to 18, took their lives, leaving that community wondering what in the world was going on. A boy and a girl, both 17, killed themselves because their parents said they couldn't see each other as often. One boy was killed in a car race; his friend, who had started the

the car race, committed suicide out of grief and guilt. Another boy killed himself out of grief over the suicide of his friend. How could it happen, in a place that has everything, where the average home costs $180,000, and where the high school football team always wins? Some of the people living there believe they know what the problem is. They explained that the only thing that counts in their community is being the best: the best at tennis, at bridge, at making money, in school. You have to have the fastest car, the biggest house, all that kind of thing. If you are not the best, you just don't count. And if you don't count, perhaps you commit suicide. Pride and envy, the demon of greatness, has ruined many lives.

It is easy for us to sit back and point a finger of condemnation at the people of Plano. We would never be as senseless as they are. Or would we? God forbid we should only condemn; God help us to learn from what happened there.

Perhaps the second cruelest demon is the unforgiving spirit that sometimes consumes us. It makes us demand absolute perfection from everyone and everything at all times. It makes us want never to be disappointed, never to be hurt, never to be let-down, never to be failed. Doctors had better never make mistakes. The driver in front of us in traffic had better get out of the way right away. If anybody or anything ever does something to let us down, well, we just won't be their friends anymore; that's all there is to it. This demon especially delights in destroying marriages. All this demon ever accomplishes is to make us frustrated and angry and lonely.

The cruelest demon of all is guilt. This nasty one hangs around us, haunting us with our past. We know better than to listen to it; we know Jesus has forgiven us all our sins; we know his blood has washed us clean; we know that in him there is now no reason for God to condemn us; we know that God no longer remembers our sins. But we remember them; we can't let them go, try as hard as we might. Guilt, like a demon, possesses us.

Jesus is God. He has power over demons. He cast seven demons out of Mary Magdalene. He has power over all the demons of our lives also. Through Word and Sacrament he brings that power to us and says to the demons in our life, "Be gone!" He says it as often as we need to hear it, over and over again, until by his power we are free from them all.

In Jesus' name. Amen

58

Epiphany 5
Mark 1:29-39

All I Need Is A Little Rest!

One of the most effective sermons I have ever preached was shared ten years ago when I was just beginning to preach. I didn't expect it to be good because I was tired when I wrote it and tired when I preached it. In fact, I was afraid I was failing the people that day because I thought the sermon wasn't much good at all.

In the sermon I shared with the folks why I was so tired, all the things that had happened to me that week. A child had died in City Hospital. The parents had no friends, no family, no one. Their doctor asked me to do the funeral. We sat together quietly in the funeral home, looking at the little lifeless body laid in a cardboard coffin. A member of the congregation I was serving as a summer vicar had suffered a near-fatal heart attack and that had taken a lot of attention. I was working forty hours a week in another job. And to top it all off, my car had blown up. I was tired, I told the people, physically, emotionally and mentally drained and the only thing holding me together was God. I shared with them how God was sustaining me. I told them that if it had not been for God I would have completely fallen apart.

The sermon came together beautifully because everybody there had been that tired sometime in their lives, most of them that very week. They knew what I was talking about because they, too, one time or another, had collapsed in God's arms for sustaining care. We came together in our common experience of exhaustion and in our shared experience of God's help. It was precious.

Being tired is something to which we can all relate. So many demands are constantly made on our time, our energy, our selves, that we regularly feel overwhelmed and worn out. Job, home, kids, marriage, other people, hobbies, telephones that keep ringing all the time: we want to shout, with the commercial, "Calgon, take me away!" People go away for a weekend just to get a little rest. Moms lock themselves up in the bathroom just to have a little peace and quiet. We lie in bed in the morning, knowing it's time to get up and get going but wishing we could just lie there a little longer. Often it seems as though we are tired most of the time.

Our Lord Jesus got that tired also. The demands that were made on him were far greater than anything that is ever asked of us, and he got very, very tired. Mark tells us that one time our Lord Jesus was so tired that "he went away to the region of Tyre and Sidon." (Mark 7:24) Jesus went into a house there to hide, to get away from everybody. He didn't want anybody to know where he was. But they found out anyway and he was not allowed to rest. Mark further tells us that Jesus was so busy he couldn't even eat in peace. (Mark 6:31) The Lord was a "man of sorrows and acquainted with grief," the One who bore the sicknesses, griefs, and sorrows of the world — the world's sin — and he was tired.

Today's Gospel lesson records for us one of those days in our Lord's life when too much happened in too little time. Our Lord's day began with a bang and kept on going that way well into the night. It was a sabbath, so Jesus went to the synagogue to worship. His quiet time in that place was shattered by a demon whom he promptly cast out. The people marveled at his power and after the worship they couldn't stop talking about what had happened. Jesus and his friends went to Peter's house for lunch. When they got there, they found Peter's mother-in-law sick with a fever. Giving us all a beautiful example of how to care for mothers-in-law, Jesus healed her. He touched her and took the fever away. News of this healing traveled as quickly as the news of the earlier healing in the synagogue and, combined, they caused all the people of the region to come to Jesus, bringing their sick and those possessed by demons. What was supposed to have been a quiet day of rest for our Lord finally ended when it was dark, and a great number of people, now healed, had been given normal, healthy lives. Then everybody left. It was time to sleep. But not for Jesus. He was too wound up and exhausted, so he went off to a lonely place and prayed.

Our Lord was always tired because the people came to him so

much. Leprous, blind, dying, crippled, they all came to him for healing. Remember the story of the man let down through the roof? Jesus was teaching in a house. The crowd was so great already that there was no more room, no way for anybody to get in. So some people peeled back the roof and with ropes lowered their crippled friend right in front of Jesus. (John 5:9) Everybody wanted a piece of the Lord. Many came, asking nothing more than to touch the fringe of his garment because those who touched it were made well. (Matthew 14:36) Great crowds followed Jesus all the time. He healed them. He fed them. He taught them. He gave them so much of himself that his own family worried about his health. Matthew tells us that the Lord's mother and brothers once came to take him home, hoping to force him to rest. (Matthew 12:46)

The reason the people mobbed Jesus that way was that he was the only One who had ever been able to help them so well. Nobody else ever did the things he did. They knew he was special. Nicodemus spoke the popular opinion when he said, "Teacher, we know that you come from God, for no one can do these signs that you do unless God is with him." (John 3:2) The people knew Jesus was special. He is special because he is God, our only Savior.

When it all got to be too much for Jesus, he went away. Six separate times the Gospels tell us that Jesus went away by himself. He especially liked to go up into the mountains. He went away and prayed. Even on the night before his death, in the closing moments before his arrest, Jesus went to be alone for a while and to pray.

What a beautiful vision of the Lord Jesus this is. He is true God, who has the power to heal all those who were brought to him. And he is true man, who got tired from overwork. He is God with us, able to sympathize with us in our experiences of life.

Like Jesus, we like to get away also when it gets to be too much. It feels good to leave all the pressure behind and go someplace. Unlike Jesus, however, we don't get as much out of our get-aways as he did because we don't do with them what he did when he went away. Jesus went away to pray. We just go away.

For our Lord, rest from all the tension of life came through prayer and quiet time with his Father in heaven. Rest came not just from "doing nothing," but from taking all that he had to do and giving it to God. Our rest comes in the same way, when we spend time with God.

Jesus frequently spent all night in prayer. It simply fascinates me that he could give up a whole night's sleep and still be refreshed in the morning. When I lose a night's sleep, I am a mess. How did he do it? His rest, his recreation came from God. So often when we are lucky enough to sleep a few extra hours or to have a few extra days off, we are still tired. David learned this fact and prayed, "Return, o my soul, to your rest." (Psalm 116:7)

We need to pray more. The more tired we are the more we need to pray. This means more than just the same old prayers we pray regularly, the mealtime prayers and the prayers we recite from memory. Good as those prayers are we need along with them to pray prayers that open up our lives to God as we give everything to him. Before choosing his disciples, Jesus prayed all night for guidance. Before he asked them, "Who do you say that I am?" he prayed all night. We have been invited by him to pray without ceasing.

Jesus said, "Come unto me all you who labor and are heavy-laden and I will give you rest." (Matthew 11:28) Just as he went to his Father for rest, we will find our rest in him also, in the Father and in our Savior. When we pour out the concerns of our life to him, telling him all that is going on, all that is making us tired, he takes those things away from us and makes the burden his own. Then it doesn't weigh us down anymore. We need to pray, to "spill out our guts" to God, to share with him our life. When we try to live it alone, without him, all we get is tired.

Jesus prayed. On the cross he prayed. While he was hanging there between heaven and earth, dying to pay for all of our sins and to make us one with God, to open up the way of communication between God and us, he prayed. "Father, into your hands I commit my spirit." His last words were a prayer. Jesus gave it all to God and God sustained him. God raised him from the dead and he lives today. He lives in us and calls us to give it all to God also, to pray so that we may finally find rest for our souls also.

And such rest may be found, in Jesus' name. Amen

Epiphany 6
Mark 1:40-45

Where's the Power?

The purveyors of "positive thinking" like to tell us that if we want something badly enough we can get it, no matter what it is. All we need is the desire, the hunger, the commitment, and if we have these three things, we can accomplish whatever we want. If we fail to achieve our goal, it is only because we didn't want it badly enough.

Positive thinking has much to recommend it, but it has its limitations. One such limitation is this: we cannot always have what we want "just because we want it." All the girls in the Miss America contest want to be Miss America but only one gets to wear the crown. The crown becomes hers not because she wanted it more than anybody else there, but because somebody gave it to her; and who in the world knows (really) how they decide which girl to give it to? They never pick the ones I like. All the young men who try to be professional athletes want to make the team, but most of them get cut because of their size, their ability or lack of it, and their injuries. All the men running for President of the United States want to be President but they get the Office, not because of their great desire for it, but rather because a majority of the voters give it to them. Just wanting to do something, to be something, to have something, is not enough to make it happen. What can happen for us is limited by the weaknesses in ourselves and in the world around us.

It is idolatry to believe that we can "do anything we want to do." We are not almighty. We are limited in power. Only God is almighty. Only God has limitless power. Only God can do whatever he wants to do. The Scriptures tell us that in God's hand are power and might. (1 Chronicles 29:12) Only with God are all things possible. (Matthew 19:26)

In his Gospel St. John tells us about a man who wanted with all his heart to be healthy but couldn't make it happen. In Jerusalem there was a pool called Bethesda. This pool was a place of healing. Every once in a while God sent an angel down into the pool to shake up the water. Whoever stepped into the pool first after the water moved was healed of whatever disease he had. A multitude of people were there, John tells us, blind, lame, paralyzed, all waiting for healing. One man had been there thirty-eight years. Jesus asked him, "Do you want to be healed?" Of course he did, but he couldn't do it because of his weakness. He told the Lord, "There is no one to help me get into the water and somebody else always gets there before me." (John 5) The man wanted to be healed but merely *desiring* it was not enough to make it happen. So Jesus healed him. Like God, Jesus has the power to do whatever he wants to do because he is God.

There's a big difference between what we can do and what God can do. Peter learned this lesson the hard way. Peter and the rest of the disciples were in a boat out on Lake Galilee. There was a storm and they were in trouble. Jesus was not with them but he saw their plight and came to them, walking on the water. When the disciples first saw him, they were scared out of their minds, thinking he was a ghost. The Lord assured them he was not. Peter asked to walk on the water with him. He wanted to walk on the water. He made it a few steps and then began to sink. His desire was not enough to keep him up. Jesus could do it because he is God and can do anything. Peter, the man, was limited by his weakness. (Matthew 14:29)

We are limited not only by our own weakness but also by weakness in the world around us and our desire cannot change that. In the Book of 1 Kings we read about a widow and her son who were powerless to do anything about their fate. They had run out of food. Everybody had run out of food. There was a famine in the land and people were dropping like flies. The widow had enough left for one meal and after she and her son ate that, they were going to lie down and die. She did not want to die; she wanted to live. She wanted to eat and to feed her son. But she couldn't make it happen. There just wasn't any food anywhere and all the wanting in the world would not change that. God fed her. For days and days and days he always gave her just enough to feed herself, her son and one guest, a prophet whom God sent to her. (1 Kings 17) We cannot do whatever we want "just because we want it." God can! "Our God does whatever he pleases," David confessed. (Psalm 115:3)

In our Gospel lesson we have a beautiful testimony to the almighty power of Jesus, our Savior, power only God has. A leper came to Jesus for healing. He wanted to be free from that ugly disease but he couldn't do anything about it. Back then nobody could do anything about it. Remember the reaction of Israel's king in our Old Testament lesson? The King of Syria sent a man to him with instructions to heal him of his leprosy. Israel's King was overwhelmed by the request. He tore his robes and asked, "Am I God, that I can heal this man?" Nobody could do anything about leprosy. The poor leper came to Jesus and, kneeling in front of the Lord, he begged for healing, saying, "If you want to, you can make me clean." The poor leper knew that Jesus had almighty power. The Lord was moved with pity and, stretching out his hand, he touched the leper and said, "I want to make you well; be clean!" And immediately he was healed. Jesus is the almighty God and he has almighty power.

"All power has been given unto me in heaven and on earth," Jesus said. (Matthew 28:18) "He was declared to be the Son of God with power by his Resurrection from the dead." (Romans 1:4) God has given him power over all flesh, power to give eternal life to all who believe in him. (John 17:2)

Confessing the almighty power of God and of our Lord Jesus Christ is not really hard to do. There is much evidence to support our confession. What is hard, however, is to understand why God doesn't use his power the way we want him to, to do the things we want him to do. If God has all power, then why do things that we consider evil still happen? Even the children are able to grasp this difficulty because they ask, "If God can do anything, why doesn't he make sin go away?" Things happen that make no sense to us at all and we sign in powerlessness, "Why doesn't God *do* something?"

There are no easy answers to such questions. We begin to understand why God does things the way he does when we learn what it is that God truly wants for us. What he wants for us is something far greater than what we typically want for ourselves.

We want to be spoiled; we want to have what we want even if it might hurt us. God wants us to be like him and with him.

The Bible tells us what God wants for us. God wants us to be his children. (John 1:13) He wants to deliver us from this present evil age. (Galatians 1:4) He wants us to be holy. (1 Thessalonians 4:3) He wants us to do right, even if we get hurt because of it. (1 Peter 2:15 and 3:17) He wants us to hope in Christ, to believe in our Savior and trust him alone and nothing (or no one) else. (Ephesians 1:11) He wants us to live with him forever. (John 14:2)

St. Paul knew there is a great difference between what we want and what God wants. Three times Paul pleaded with God about the same thing, asking to be healed of his "thorn in the flesh." Three times he was turned down. Still, the Apostle confessed, "The will of God is good and perfect and acceptable." (Romans 12:2) Things happen and God appears to do nothing about it because he doesn't do what we want him to do. God does do something; he does what he wants, what he knows will make his greatest wish for us happen: our salvation.

Because we are God's children who know he loves us and has made us his own, we accept what he wants for us even though it hurts sometimes. We pray in our prayers, "thy will be done," just as our Lord Jesus himself prayed it. Jesus of Nazareth, the man, was powerless in his weakness to do anything but to place himself in his Father's care. He didn't want to die but he knew he had to, so he prayed, "Not my will but thine be done." Not what I want, Father, but what you want. What God wanted is exactly what happened. Jesus died, and because of it we are saved. Jesus came back to life again and because of it we have a home in heaven. By doing it God's way, accepting what God wanted, Jesus was glorified and now his name is greater than any other name, a name at which every knee will bow in heaven, on earth and under the earth. What God wanted for Jesus was best for him and also for us. What God wants for us is best for us also, even when we can't see it. To do what is best for us is that for which God uses his almighty power.

Through Jesus he brings his power into our lives. Amen

Epiphany 7
Mark 2:1-12

Who Does He Think He Is?

"Who in the world does he think he is?" was the question buzzing around in the threatened little minds of the scribes in our Gospel lesson. Jesus had just spoken forgiveness of sins to a man and he had said it as if he really meant it! The scribes immediately took offense. "Only God can do that!" they said to themselves. "Who does he think he is, anyway?" As our Lord carried out his ministry of healing, teaching, forgiving and loving, that came more and more to be the question about him.

The people were divided in their opinions about him. Some said, "He is a good man," while others said, "No, he is leading the people astray." (John 7:12) The religious leaders of the day condemned him saying, "This man is not from God for he does not keep the Sabbath." What they meant was that he did not obey the rules the way they wanted him to, the way their tradition taught. But others said, "How can a man who is a sinner do such great signs?" (John 9:16) His severest critics dismissed him with, "He has a demon and he is mad!" But his defenders countered, "These are not the sayings of one who has a demon; can a demon open the eyes of the blind?" (John 10:19)

With each passing day, every new miracle, every godly lesson and every loving act of mercy, opinions about the Lord became more and more definite. Lines were drawn. Many, like the disciples, stricken by all the evidence, came to confess about him, "You are the Christ, the Son of the Living God." Many others, unwilling to admit that he was right because of all the changes that would call for in their own lives, rejected him, refusing to believe in him.

Who did he think he was, anyway? The Gospels record for us our Lord's own testimony. This is what Jesus said about himself: "I am the Way, the Truth and the Life; no one comes to the Father but by me." (John 14:6) "I am the Bread of Life which came down from heaven." (John 6:41, 48) "I am the Light of the world; whoever follows me will not walk in darkness but will have the light of life." (John 8:12) "I am the Door; all who enter in by me will be saved . . . I came that you may have life and have it abundantly; I am the Good Shepherd; the Good Shepherd lays down his life for the sheep." (John 10:9, 10, 11) "I am the Resurrection and the Life; whoever believes in me, though he die, yet shall he live and whoever lives and believes in me shall never die." (John 11:25) Jesus clearly thought that he was the Messiah, the Christ, true God. "I and the Father are one," he said. (John 10:30)

The people — believers and unbelievers alike — got this message very clearly. St. John tells us of three separate attempts on the life of our Lord before his crucifixion. (John 5:18; 8:58; 10:31) All three times his enemies tried to kill him because he tried to make himself equal with God, they said. Our Lord succeeded very well in letting everyone know who he thought he was. Precisely because of his claims, they finally did kill him.

Jesus thought he was God and said so. Just thinking he was God, however, was not enough to make it true. He was not the only one of his day claiming to be the Messiah. There were many others, even during his lifetime, and since then many more, who have claimed to be God. That kind of thing still happens. Look at Mr. Moon and how his "moonies" believe in him.

On the TV show, "Mash," a few years back there was a soldier who believed that he was Jesus Christ and told everybody so. He had been traumatized in battle because of all the killing he had done and, to escape from himself, he assumed the identity of Jesus. Sydney, the psychiatrist, couldn't do anything to change his mind about it. The soldier was so convinced in his delusion that Radar began to believe it too, and received a blessing for himself and for his teddy bear.

The emperors of Rome delighted in calling themselves "god." Domitian, especially, was consumed with his divinity. An ancient historian recorded that it was dangerous to talk about the weather with Domitian. As "god" he considered himself personally responsible for the weather and if one said it was bad he took it as a personal insult. In his reign, crimes against the state were labeled "godlessness."

By themselves, then, our Lord's words about himself would not be enough to persuade us of his godhood. The Savior knew this. He said, "If you don't believe *me,* at least believe the *works* that I do that you may know and understand that the Father is in me and I am in the Father." (John 10:38) Jesus didn't only *say* he was God; he *acted* like it, doing things that only God can do. And it was those deeds that persuaded the people, for they asked in sheer wonder, "When the Christ comes, will he do more signs than this man has done?" (John 7:31) How could he? Jesus did it all: healing, casting out demons, controlling nature, raising the dead, even coming back to life again himself. Many have claimed to be the Christ; many have presented themselves as "god." Only one of them all has ever died and come back to life again.

Of all the divine works of Jesus, the one most definitive sign of his godhood is the way he forgave sins. The scribes were right when they said, "Only God can forgive sins!" Jesus did it because he is God. By his own power he forgives sins.

And does he forgive! He forgave the thief dying on the cross next to his own. He forgave the woman caught in adultery. He forgave the dishonest tax collectors. He forgave the prostitutes. He forgave the woman who had been married six times. He even forgave Peter, who had betrayed him three times, swearing he didn't know the Man. Jesus forgives sin. He forgave those who nailed him to the cross. All we can do about sin is make excuses for it or ignore it entirely, pretending it isn't real, or be burdened by it with great guilt. Jesus takes sin away. "If we confess our sins," John wrote, Jesus "is faithful and just to forgive us our sins" *and to clean up the mess of our wrongdoing.* (1 John 1:9)

It's hard to *see* the forgiveness of sins and even harder to *believe* it. How can we know that Jesus really forgives us all our sins? How can we tell when we are forgiven? Is it possible to know for sure that one's sins are forgiven? Jesus gives us the answer by giving us something we can see. After forgiving the sins of the paralytic, he asked the people there, "What's harder to do? To forgive sins or to make a cripple walk?" That's a good question, isn't it? Both are far beyond our ability; both are humanly impossible; both require a miracle; both take God's power. So, Jesus said, "To let you know that I do have power to forgive sins," he said to the paralytic, "Get up and walk!" And immediately he walked. Jesus does the impossible, even forgiving our sins. We can believe it, even though we can't see it.

When Jesus says, "I forgive your sins," there is saving action behind those words. "This is my blood of the New Testament," Jesus said, "which is poured out for you for the forgiveness of sins." (Matthew 26:28) Forgiveness of sins is ours not only in the words of Jesus, but in his life, death and Resurrection, the actions of forgiveness. "In him," Paul wrote, "we have redemption through his blood, the forgiveness of sins according to the riches of his grace." (Ephesians 1:7)

Jesus knows who he is. He is the Christ, the Son of God, the Savior of the world. He proved that with his words and his deeds. For all who know who they are — sinners needing grace — and believe in him, he is the greatest good there can be: forgiveness of sins, life and salvation.

They are all ours, in Jesus' name. Amen

Epiphany 8
Mark 2:18-22

How Can You Tell
When People Are Religious?

For seven days King David fasted. Day and night he went without food as he prayed desperately for the life of his newborn child. The baby had been born as a result of his affair with Bathsheba, an adulterous affair that had led to the murder of Bathsheba's husband. From the moment the baby was born, it was evident the child's life was hanging by a slim thread. So David prayed for the life of the child. He prayed with great intensity. He fasted as part of his prayers, hoping that by his petitions and by his avoidance of food he could make God be gracious to him and let the child live. But on the seventh day, in spite of the King's hunger and all his prayers, the baby died.

Fasting, such as King David did, used to be a regular part of religion. People fasted as a sign of sorrow over their sins. People fasted in grief over the death of a loved one. People fasted when they prayed about something important. They fasted to excite the pity and compassion of God.

In the book of Jonah we read about a whole city that fasted. God sent Jonah to the cruel and wicked city of Nineveh to proclaim to them their sins and God's anger with them. After Jonah preached his message of divine destruction, all the people, from the king on down to the littlest person in the city, hundreds of thousands of people, all repented. As a sign of their repentance, their sorrow over their sins, the whole city fasted. They went without both food and water because they wanted to show God that they had turned from their evil ways.

God only commanded fasting for one day of the year, and only for the Hebrew people. On the Day of Atonement, a day of national repentance and confession of sin, God wanted all the people of Israel to fast. But aside from that one day, God nowhere else commanded general fasting. Nevertheless, people began to fast for a number of different reasons and at any given time. We read in the Bible that Moses fasted; so did Elijah, Ezra and Daniel.

Today, if people fast at all, only rarely does it happen as part of their religion. Today people fast when they are on a diet or they fast to protest something. Some IRA revolutionaries fasted themselves to death some time ago, as a protest to conditions they found unacceptable. Ghandi was an expert at fasting; through his hunger strikes he was able to effect a number of changes in his country. While God has not commanded Christians to fast, for some people it is a good thing to do. Our Lord Jesus fasted; so did St. Paul and many others in the early Christian Church. They fasted as part of their faith relationship with God.

By the time of Jesus, fasting had grown to be nothing more than a tradition for most people. There came to be a great deal of fasting but it was not connected to a healthy fear of God. People fasted mostly to show off how religious they were. Our Savior told a story about a Pharisee who fasted for this reason. Remember the parable of the Pharisee who went to the Temple to pray? He prayed a proud prayer, Jesus tells us, in which he boasted to God of all the good things he did. As part of his self-righteous list he bragged, ". . . I fast twice a week! . . . " (Luke 18:9-14) God was not pleased with his fast nor with most fasting that went on because people fasted for themselves but not for him. Because their fasts were seldom faith-full, God said through Jeremiah, "Though they fast, I will not hear their cry . . . but I will consume them . . . " (Jeremiah 14:12)

Since fasting was a way of measuring how religious a person was, Jesus and his disciples were criticized by some because they didn't fast. They didn't act "religious enough." "Why do the disciples of John the Baptizer and the disciples of the Pharisees fast?" the people asked Jesus, "But your disciples don't fast?" Matthew tells us this question bothered not only the general public, but the disciples of John especially. They didn't like the idea that, while their stomachs growled because they were empty, the stomachs of the disciples of our Lord were full and content.

Jesus explained that his disciples didn't fast because there was no reason for them to fast while he was around. Jesus wrapped his answer in the imagery of a wedding reception. He called himself a bridegroom. Just as the mood of a wedding reception is one of gaiety and joy, so also the mood of the followers of Jesus is to be full of joy. The mood of a fast is like the mood of a funeral and that's just not an appropriate mood for Christians.

Remember, fasting happened as a response to grief when a loved one died, out of remorse over sin, as a way to make God listen to prayer and (for most people) to show off their religion. For the Christian, Jesus says, there is no reason to act that way. Where there is death, Jesus Christ gives life! Where there is guilt and separation from God, Jesus Christ brings forgiveness and oneness with the Father! Jesus has opened up the way of communication between God and us, and we don't have to make God listen to our prayers any more; he listens just because of Jesus! And most of all, Christians don't go around trying to prove how good they are; they trust Jesus who has made them good already, through his own righteous life, death and resurrection.

This last point was the real concern behind the question of the people. They wanted to know, "How can you tell when people are religious?" With fasting and other such outward practices it's very easy to tell who the "religious" folks are. They are the ones who have deep circles around their eyes from lying awake at night thinking about food. They are the ones who break into a cold sweat everytime somebody mentions food.

But the truth is, it's not always easy to know who the religious people are. Perhaps a better way to say that would be, just because people look religious does not mean they are close to God; and the opposite is also true. In the days of Jesus one could see people giving alms to the poor in the Temple and on the streets; one could hear people praying aloud in public; and one could see people walking around with long faces because they were hungry from fasting. Jesus called them all hypocrites. (Matthew 6) He condemned them because everything they did was done to show off, to impress people. Jesus said, in response to their irreligion, "When you do your good works . . . when you give alms, when you pray and when you fast, do it in secret so no one sees you but God and he will reward you." (Matthew 6)

How can you tell who the really religious people are? We can't always tell because the truly faithful do what they do not to impress us but simply because they love God. That's something that happens in the heart — and how can one look into someone's heart? For this reason, Jesus told us to be very careful about judging others.

Religion that happens in the heart first and then on the sleeve was a very new teaching for the people who heard the Lord. It required changes in the way they thought about their religion and some people hate it when changes are made. Jesus admitted it was a new teaching. He called it, "new wine for fresh skins." It was all part of the new covenant, the new agreement, he came to make between God and humanity. Our Lord's new covenant is a covenant built not on what people do but on what he has done and keeps on doing for us and on what we believe. The covenant depends on Jesus Christ alone. "This is *my* blood of the new covenant," Jesus said, explaining how it happens.

What counts is not what we do but what Jesus Christ does for us and in us and that we believe in him. The January 1984 issue of the *Lutheran Witness* had an article that powerfully illustrates this truth. It's the story of the Good Shepherd Lutheran Mission in Kansas City. The people of that ghetto church would not measure up to being religious by anyone's standards. Every single girl in the parish over fifteen years of age has at least one child of her own. One woman in the Bible Class set fire to her neighbor's house to cover the evidence of her break-in to steal from her neighbor. The law of their community is that if it's not nailed down, it's going to walk; if it is stolen it's your fault for not taking better care of it. Like most people in the ghetto, these people have to scratch and claw to stay alive — and they do. Are they religious? They say they believe in God; they worship him and they study his Word. Are they religious? Are they any worse than the nice people who gossip and "fudge" on their taxes and flirt with the god of money? What makes people truly religious is Jesus Christ and their faith in him. That's all.

In that same article, the pastor asked a disturbingly provocative question. Remembering the way Jesus treated the woman who had been caught in adultery he asked, "If you were the pastor and you were at the altar of your church, holding the host and the chalice in your hands, ready for Holy Communion, and there before you knelt a woman whom you knew for certain did not spend the night alone . . . what would you do?'' The pastor went on to answer his own question: "Jesus said, "I don't condemn you; go and sin no more." The Church can do no less.

We need to be careful that we never fall into the trap of thinking the way the Pharisees thought, that we are better or more religious than some other folks because we don't do the same bad things they do. We are all sinners and we are all good only by grace through faith in Jesus Christ alone. Amen

The Transfiguration
Mark 9:2-9

Butterflies and Jesus

As I was working on my sermon this past week I toyed with the idea of bringing a live butterfly along with me to church this morning so I could let it go right about now, as an attention getter. I decided against doing that, however, because I was afraid it would get your attention so well that I might never get it back again. I had visions of all of you sitting out there spending the rest of the service distracted as you followed the butterfly around, your heads bobbing up and down after it. So I brought along the next best thing instead, a pinned butterfly. It's much easier to control.

This is a beautiful butterfly, isn't it? By and large, people don't like bugs very well, but almost everybody makes an exception for butterflies because they are so beautiful. As you all know, a butterfly hasn't always been beautiful. For the first part of its life it was a caterpillar, a wooly worm crawling around on the ground looking (in some people's opinion) gross. But at a special time and in a spectacular fashion, the ugly, little, wooly worm got transformed into a beautiful butterfly. When one looks at a lowly caterpillar crawling around, it's hard to believe that a beautiful butterfly, able to fly all over on light and colorful wings, could be inside of it. But it is! This transformation from caterpillar to butterfly is something we call a *metamorphosis.*

The word metamorphosis has the same root in the Greek language as the word *Transfiguration,* the word we use to describe what happened to Jesus in our text today. This is the story of how Jesus "acted like a butterfly," if you will, and was metamorphosed into glory right before his disciples' eyes. Peter, James and John saw Jesus in all of his glory, the glory of the only-begotten Son of God.

The story of the Transfiguration is one of the least-known stories about Jesus. Everybody hears hundreds of times about the Lord's birth, death and Resurrection, but very few people ever get to know the details of the Transfiguration. Even in art, this great event gets passed over. Unlike other events in our Lord's life which frequently become the subject of art, there are less than a handful of works of art to depict the Transfiguration. From the sixth and eighth centuries we have some mosaics that hint at it. And of the great masters, only the artist Raphael attempted to paint the Transfiguration. His painting hangs in the Vatican, but Raphael died before he could finish the job. It's almost as if there's a message there that no human art or genius, tongue or pen, can do justice in representing the spectacular event that happened when Jesus was transfigured.

What happened at the Transfiguration is that Jesus' physical body was metamorphosed into his spiritual, godly person. Mark tells us the Lord's garments became intensely, glistening white, like nothing else on earth could ever be. They were far brighter than the snow is on a sunny day, when your eyes burn from looking at it. This description of our Lord's appearance matches identically the description of the appearance of the angel who announced the Resurrection. Jesus had a heavenly appearance about him. Matthew tells us not only his clothes were shining, but his face also shone like the sun itself, not reflecting light, but with a tremendous light streaming out from it. For a time, Jesus was completely enveloped by the fulness of his godhood, right before the eyes of three disciples. No wonder our text tells us those fortunate men were afraid. They were tremendously impressed: they were dazzled by the glory of Jesus.

It's an awesome thing to see the glory of God. We read in the Old Testament that Moses asked God for permission to see the divine glory when he was up on Mt. Sinai. God said to him, "I will let you see the back side of me, but you cannot see my face; for no one can see me and live." (Exodus 33:17-23) God then told Moses to hide himself in the cleft of a rock and to hide his face while God passed by. In spite of all the precautions that were taken, even though Moses was exposed to only a little of the majesty of God, still, his face shone so brightly from the experience that the people could not stand to look at him. He had to wear a veil over his face to darken the glow. Such an experience is what Jesus shared with his three disciples.

The message of the Transfiguration is that Jesus Christ is God. Contrary to all those who say he was only a great man, or just a great prophet, or who say even less than that about him, the Gospels tell us — and we believe — that Jesus is God. "Without controversy," St. Paul wrote, "great is the mystery of our religion: God was manifest in the flesh, justified in the Spirit, seen of angels, preached unto the Gentiles, believed on in the world and received up into glory." (1 Timothy 3:16)

The deity of our Lord has always been questioned and doubted. Even the disciples were slow to come around, slow to know him in truth. St. John recorded for us an incident which happened shortly before our Lord's death, one that shows how unsure the disciples still were of the Lord's true identity. Jesus told them, "I go to prepare a place for you." In response to this great good news, Thomas said, "Lord, we don't know where you are going, how can we know the way?" and Philip added, "Lord, show us the Father and we will be satisfied!" In great frustration, Jesus said to him, "Have I been with you so long and yet you do not know me, Philip?" He who has seen me has seen the Father; how can you say, 'Show us the Father?' Don't you believe that I am in the Father and the Father is in me?" To Thomas Jesus said, "I am the Way, the Truth and the Life." (John 14:1-11)

On several occasions the Lord testified to his Godhood. "I and the Father are one," he said. (John 10:30) "All things that the Father has are mine," he added. (John 16:15) And on the night before he died, he prayed, "Father, glorify me now with the glory which I had with you before the world was." (John 17:5)

The enemies of our Lord heard his confessions about himself and understood clearly what he was saying. He told them, "Before Abraham was, I am . . . " They knew he called himself God and because of it they kept trying to kill him until they finally succeeded. He died, but he came back to life again, proving with power to rise from the dead that he is God. (Romans 1:4) St. Paul said it well when he wrote, "In him dwells all the fulness of God bodily." (Colossians 2:9) St. John said it perfectly when he wrote, "In the beginning was the Word and the Word was with God and the Word was God." (John 1:1)

We joyfully confess that Jesus is God because it means that we have a perfect Savior. If Jesus had been anything less than God, then he would not have been good enough, nor could he have done enough for our salvation to come true. Mere humans, dying for their sins, do nothing to merit God's forgiveness. But Jesus is God and because of it he is our perfect Savior. "By the obedience of this one person, all who believe in him are made righteous." (Romans 5:19) By his one, solitary life and death, all the sins of the world are paid for. By his death and Resurrection, death and hell are overcome for all who believe in him; eternal life is ours. "Thanks be to God," St. Paul wrote, "who gives us the victory through our Lord Jesus Christ." (1 Corinthians 15:57)

Earlier I made reference to some mosaics of the sixth century that hint at the Transfiguration of our Lord. One of those mosaics is at the Basilica of Ravenna. This mosaic particularly connnects the Transfiguration of our Lord with our salvation. In the mosaic there is a jeweled cross set in a circle of blue with golden stars. At the very center is the face of Jesus, our Savior. From a cloud close by, a hand reaches out, symbolizing God's voice, and points to the cross. The message of the mosaic appears to be that at the moment of the Transfiguration, God spoke to his Son and pointed him to the cross, to his mission in life. God called his Son to die in payment for the sins of the world so that the world might be saved.

Peter, James and John saw Jesus in his glory. They were the privileged three who shared in so many extraordinary experiences with the Lord. They were there when Jesus brought Jairus' little girl back to life again. They were there also with Jesus in the Garden of Gethsemane when Jesus asked them to pray with him. They were there on the mountain when Jesus was in his glory. Peter was beside himself because of the moment. He didn't know what to say, but he said what he felt: "Lord, it's good for us to be here ..."

One gets the feeling that what Peter felt in that moment was similar to the feelings described by some people who die momentarily and are brought back to life again. The experiences of what we now call "life after life." To be honest with you, I am very skeptical of those reports and I don't think we should put much stock in them. Yet, some people report experiencing feelings of great peace and tranquility. They feel so good on "the other side" that they are angry for being brought back to life again. That's how Peter felt up on that mountain. It was good to be there; he wanted to stay up there forever; he didn't want to come back down ever again.

With Peter we also confess that it is good to be with Jesus in his glory. It is good to know who he is: The Christ, the Son of the Living God, *my* Lord and Savior. It is so good to know him that we don't ever want to turn back from knowing him. We never want to go away from his glory.

Recently I heard a beautiful confession of faith from one of our members. This member has not been a Christian long and to hear him confess his faith so powerfully absolutely thrilled me. He said, "If my Christian faith has done nothing else for me, it has definitely filled me with an inner peace and serenity that I never had before. I know that I am in the hands of God and that whatever happens to me is part of God's Grand Plan. I don't worry about what happens. If I go to the poor house, that's okay; if I go the other way, that's okay. I do my best, but it's really God who takes care of me." What a beautiful confession of faith. Just like Peter's, "It's good, Lord, to be here."

Sometimes I wonder how well we know what is good for us. From some of the things we do to ourselves one can get the distinct impression that we do not know what is good. Just recently I heard from a psychologist that the formula for success in our society is the classical formula for a nervous breakdown as described by psychiatry. We complain about our lives but we do nothing about them. We keep on spending and rushing and moving and doing. We keep on looking for what is good for us but we never seem to find it or to be satisfied with what good we find. People move in and out of houses, cities, cars, jobs, marriages, sometimes even life itself, hoping the next one will be good. But all we ever seem to find is what we left behind.

In all this confusion, there is one true good, the greatest good of all. "It is good, Lord, to be here . . . " Jesus is our greatest good. The more we look to him for good in our life and the less we look in all the wrong places, the more good we will find; the more good we will have. St. James explained why: "Every good endowment and every perfect gift is from above, coming down from the Father of lights . . . " (James 1:17)

Guess what! The good never ends. The metamorphosis that happened to Jesus is happening to us also. It's true! In our Epistle lesson we read, "All who reflect the glory of the Lord are being changed into his likeness from one degree to another . . . " (2

Corinthians 3:18) You and I, all who believe in Jesus, are going to be in glory also, all because of Jesus, our God and Savior, who is the greatest good for us, now and forever. That's worth celebrating, in his precious name. Amen